World Trade

World Trade

◆

A Network Approach

Bernard C. Beaudreau

iUniverse, Inc.
New York Lincoln Shanghai

World Trade
A Network Approach

iUniverse, Inc.

For information address:
iUniverse, Inc.
2021 Pine Lake Road, Suite 100
Lincoln, NE 68512
www.iuniverse.com

ISBN: 0-595-33054-1

Printed in the United States of America

Contents

Preface vii

CHAPTER 1   Introduction 1

CHAPTER 2   Trade and Networks 10

CHAPTER 3   The Theory of Network Trade 41

CHAPTER 4   A Model of Vertical Trade. 69

CHAPTER 5   International Trade: The Evidence 88

CHAPTER 6   Trade Policy: A Network Approach. 113

CHAPTER 7   Trade and Networks: Implications and
             Consequences 132

CHAPTER 8   Summary and Conclusions 147

Endnotes. 151

Bibliography 159

Preface

What started as an attempt on my part to integrate the concept of networks into the theory of international trade soon took on a life of its own, culminating in a treatise on the role of networks in trade in general. Starting with my interest in ancient empires and multinational firms, I initially set out to integrate networks and network structure into international trade theory. This proved considerably more demanding than originally thought. Getting in the way of such an integration was the lack of a theory of networks that was sufficiently general to lend itself to the study of international trade. Unfortunately, research on networks in economics is currently at the embryonic stage, with few testable predictions, and even fewer applications. Not helping matters is the fact that in this literature, networks are assumed, not derived. More to the point, it is assumed that to trade, agents must pay a fee (network cost).

Feeling that such an approach fails to adequately capture the essence of trade networks, whether archaeologically, historically, or empirically, I began reexamining the theoretical bases of networks. The result is this book which should be seen as a multidisciplinary approach to trade and networks, one that, I feel, provides a more compelling theory of the underpinnings of networks, and their evolution over time.

I would like to thank all those who over the years provided valuable feedback on earlier drafts. I would especially like to thank Meagan Daley, for the countless hours spent discussing neuroscience and networks, and my students (undergraduate and graduate) who over the years served as sounding boards for many of the ideas presented here. All errors and omissions, however, remain my sole responsibility.

1

Introduction

Trade has, since time immemorial, been conducted in well-defined networks. The Roman Empire, the British Empire, NAFTA, and the European Union are examples. In ancient Rome, raw materials (including slaves) and foodstuffs were imported from Northern African colonies, which, in return, imported finished goods and Roman colonial administration. In 18th century Britain, furs were imported from its colonies in return for finished goods. Academics exchange ideas in well-defined networks (associations and journals). Today, goods, services, and capital flow freely between Canada, the United States and Mexico, the result of the North American Free Trade Agreement (NAFTA); similarly, goods, service, capital and labor flow freely between the member countries of the European Union.[1]

Socially, we as a species trade within the well-defined networks, be they one's family, one's circle of friends, or one's work environment. Despite few impediments to trade outside of these networks, we typically restrict our exchange activity to is our networks. In short, we as a species trade (exchange) in well-defined, relatively-stable networks.

Unfortunately, the theory of trade in economics is devoid of networks. Instead, trade is carried out in markets, where impersonal buyers and sellers interact indirectly via a fictitious auctioneer. Networks are altogether absent. This is not altogether surprising given the underlying micro-foundations, specifically, the theory of the consumer, and the theory of the producer. Take, for example, the theory of the consumer, where the underlying view of Homo sapiens-sapiens behavior is liimited and limiting—in short, where our species a mere shadow of itself. Homo-oeconomicus, is seen as an insatiable consumer of goods and services, and leisure (averse to work). All higher-order human needs as found in the other social sciences such as psychology and sociology are absent. In fact, one could argue that consumer theory is not about Homo sapiens-sapiens, but rather

1

about some lower-order primate. Producer theory suffers from similar shortcomings (see Beaudreau (1998,1999)).

We know, however, that there is more to Homo sapiens-sapiens than the standard Arrow-Debreu agent. For example, we know that our species is fundamentally social—in fact, it is well-known that we are the most social of all primates. We live and work in groups (networks), we trade in well-defined groups (networks), and we consume in well-defined groups (networks). A number of recent developments in economics speak to these differences. For example, George Akerlof and Rachel Kranton, in recent work, have begun to examine the role of identity in behavior (Akerlof and Kranton 2000). Others have begun to examine the role of socialization in behavior (Jackson 2003).

Clearly, what is needed is a more complete theory of consumer behavior, one that incorporates lower-order as well as higher-order needs. Such a theory would mirror the complexity of the human experience, and speak to the higher-order needs of our species. In addition, it would provide the micro-foundations for a theory of social behavior, networks, and ultimately, a network theory of trade.

Admittedly, this is a tall order, one that no one paper, article or book can fill. The past five years have witnessed an explosion in work on networks in economics. These are discussed in Chapter 3. Finding this literature to be somewhat restricted in its approach to understanding networks, both historically and theoretically, and wanting to provide a multidisciplinary approach to the study of networks in economics, I present, in this book, a network approach to world trade, one that is considerably broader in scope. Instead of analyzing network formation in what is otherwise a market-based framework, I derive networks from first principles, the latter consisting of the basic axioms of human evolution as found in the archaeological record.

The book is organized around a number of key principles, notably the notion of consilience, or seamless science. For example, it will be argued that networks are universal in form and function. As such, the economic theory of networks has to, at the very least, be consilient with the biological theory of networks, as well as the sociological theory of networks. Another is the relative importance of the archaeological and historical record in theoretical work. The purpose of network theory is not to construct models of fictitious networks—although this may be used as a means—but rather is to explain human behavior, past, present and future.

Over the course of the next six chapters, an attempt will be made to better understand the role of networks in trade activity. Among the various issues examined are the role of information in trade activity, with particular attention on the role of information processing, storage and retrieval in all forms of social activity, including trade (goods and services). Another important question is the role networks played in the rise of large-scale specialization and trade (6,000BCE). The archeological record shows that early civilizations were organized around well-defined networks in which citizenship constituted the basis for membership. Theoretically, it is shown that networking and trade are intimately linked to information, specifically, the ability to process (transmit, store and retrieve) information. In ancient times (pre-civilization), the ability to network and trade was an increasing function of a specie's ability to process information in the cortex (neo-pallium). Species with larger cortexes, the evolutionary record shows, were more social, that is, had larger networks, and engaged in more trade (social and economic).

Social and economic networks remained relatively stable for thousands of years (until the Neolithic era). Then, roughly 8,000 years ago, new network forms appeared, in the form of large city-states, with over 10,000 members. This raises a number of interesting theoretical questions, notably, why and how? Why did Homo-sapiens sapiens begin to network on a large-scale? Why did city-states replace villages (agglomerations) that had no more than a few hundred members? What were the associated information requirements? At issue here is perhaps one of the most fundamental questions in the human experience, namely, the rise of civilization as we know it today. What factors prompted this revolutionary change? Was civilization a spontaneous occurrence—that is, the result of optimizing behavior on the part of individual agents, or was it the result of coordinated action? Did the resulting large-scale specialization and exchange arise as a result of individual choices, or collective choices. It is generally believed that complex economic and social organization emerged spontaneously. I take issue with this view. Theoretically, I show that large-scale, organized trade is highly unlikely to have arisen spontaneously.[2]

Specifically, I show that the equilibrium to the corresponding Nash autarky-specialize game is a state of autarky; that is, individual agents have no private incentives to specialize. This result is formalized in terms of two Spontaneous Trade Impossibility Theorems.

That large-scale specialization and exchange was not a spontaneous occurrence (Nash equilibrium) raises what I believe is a puzzle, namely that if, in fact, this is true, then how can one explain the rise of civilization, the defining feature of which is large-scale specialization and exchange? Drawing from the historical record, specifically, the history of the ancient world, I show that the emergence of large-scale public-choice mechanisms, motivated by the existence of large-scale public goods, contributed in a non-negligible way to resolving the underlying coordination failure (i.e. of the corresponding Nash game), and, in so doing, contributed to the emergence of large-scale specialization and exchange, which, I go on to argue, dates back to ancient Sumer.[3] The existence of a large-scale public good (e.g. ziggurat) led to what I refer to as public choice-based specialization and exchange, where public goods (religious services) were exchanged, via taxation, against various other goods and services. This, I argue, led to the emergence of secondary trades (markets) in which agents traded spontaneously among themselves. Historically, the record shows that this activity was typically carried out in close geographical proximity to the public good (e.g. ziggurat, palace, church).

The genesis of specialization and exchange, notably, the presence of public-choice mechanisms and, consequently, public goods, I go on to argue, had a non-negligible effect on the very nature of the ensuing trade. Specifically, large-scale trade was, from the very beginning, conducted in well-defined political (geopolitical) networks. Internal—to the political network—trade was encouraged, while external trade (foreign trade) was discouraged. The reason was relatively straightforward, namely the classical free-rider problem. As the public good(s) was(were) responsible for the making of markets, it stands to reason that everyone had to bear the cost. Foreigners, not being obliged to pay taxes in the country, would, in the absence of barriers to trade, be classic free-riders. That is, enjoy the fruits of market activity, without having contributed.

This, I argue, helps explain why trade, from ancient Sumer to the present, has been carried out in well-defined geopolitical networks (e.g. city-states, nations, countries, federations), and why extra-network (foreign) trade has, until recently, been either illegal, or been discouraged (barriers to trade). Governments have, from the start, been responsible for the emergence of large-scale specialization and trade, making for a situation in which free trade—or the absence of barriers—raises the free-rider problem, which, if left unchecked, can, at least potentially, lead to the demise of government, and, in the limiting case, to the demise of markets.

The history of trade, I argue, is, in essence, the history of large-scale specialization and exchange within well-defined geopolitical networks, sometimes referred to as empires, countries, federations, and nation-states. The ancient and modern historical record shows that geopolitical networks are fungible, expanding or contracting over time. As I shall attempt to show, underlying the growth (fusion and fission) of geopolitical networks has been, and continues to be, the most important source of gains from trade, historically speaking, namely the exchange of raw materials for value added. This is referred to as vertical trade. Within geopolitical networks, raw material-producing regions trade with manufacturing regions, the former exporting raw materials (processed), and the latter exporting value added. The Roman empire is a case in point, being a geopolitical trade network in which raw-materials (including slaves) flowed to Rome, in return for finished goods.

Table 1.1
The Challand-Rageau List of Empires

Sumer and the First Empires
The Assyrian Empire
The Acheminde Empire
Athens and the Greek World
Alexander the Great
The Mauryan Empire
The Chinese Empire under the Han
The Roman Empire
The Justinian Empire
The Sassanide Empire-Iran
The Empire of the Omeyyades
The Tang Chinese Empire
The Abbassides Empire
Charlemagne's Empire
The Byzantine Empire
The Seldjoukide Empire

Source: Chaliland and Rageau (1993).

As I will argue, free trade (extra network) is welfare-reducing owing to the free-rider problem. Foreigners benefit from markets (specialization and exchange) without contributing. This explains why extra-network trade was forbidden in ancient economies. This raises a fundamental question, namely, why did Great Britain in the 19th century, and the United States in the 20th century, two well-established, successful networks, revoke 6,000 years of network trade (a defining feature of which is protectionism), and adopt what were essentially free-trade policies? It is important to recall that up until then, both had been staunch opponents of free trade.

Britain turned its back on protection in 1846, when it repealed the Corn Laws, and adopted imperial preference, the keystone of which was the most-favored-nation principle. Accordingly, any tariff concession made to one of Great Britain's trading partner, would apply automatically to all other partners. The United States turned its back on protection in 1934 with the passage of the

Reciprocal Trade Agreements Act, empowering the executive branch of the government with the authority to negotiate reciprocal trade agreements.

Both, I argue, can be understood in terms of networks, specifically, in terms of network dynamics. Networks exist in space in time, organizing economic (production and distribution) activity. Changes in technology and/or tastes can and will alter the optimal configuration of the network. Previous trading patterns, once optimal, will, as such, no longer be, prompting calls for change. Also, institutional innovations, notably the emergence of transnational firms, altered the nature of the problem.

For example, the decision, on the part of Great Britain, to abandon traditional network trade (colonial policy) in favor of "free-trade," should be understood as resulting from (*i*) a technology shock, (*ii*) the escalating cost of imperial wars, and (*iii*) the emergence of British transnational corporations. The steam engine rendered Great Britain's 18th century colonial empire redundant, unable to provide the necessary feed-stocks, the most important of which was cotton—and later, silk. The market for furs and pelts had collapsed. Having lost the thirteen colonies in 1776, its could do either of two things. It could either (*i*) invade the United States in the hope of re-annexing it to the empire, or (*ii*) advocate a new form of trading arrangement, one that was based purely on gains from trade, and one divorced from geopolitical issues—in short, what became known as free trade.

The imperial wars had exacted a heavy toll (French and Indian War) on Great Britain, emptying the treasury. This, in combination with the military strength of the United States, all but put an end to Britain's imperial aspirations, forcing it to reinvent the geopolitical-economic network of old, the result of which was the doctrine of free trade as we know it today. According to its chief architects, foreign trade would hitherto be free of government.

> One Whig, speaking before the House of Commons during the Corn Law debate of 1846, described free trade as the beneficent principle by which foreign nations would become valuable colonies to us, without imposing on us the responsibility of governing them. (Semmel 1970, 8)

Clearly, what Great Britain had in mind was a global trade network, with England at the center. Mediating trade would be the new privately-held networks that were the joint-stock companies such as the Dutch East-India Company. Other nations (formerly colonies) would via private, British-based networks, provide the necessary feed-stocks, that would be transformed in England. The cost of such a network would be negligible. Redundant colonies could be simply abandoned, at little-to-no cost to the crown. Wealth could be amassed without incurring the prohibitive costs (administrative) of the former empires.

> The industry and energy of this country under her colonial system were made to feed and increase her home manufactures. That illiberal and hostile policy which the mother country displayed to her colonies in our early history has been steadfastly pursued by her from that day to this. Whatever advancement has been made by American manufacturers has been over the protest and in spite of the piratical rivalry of, that great manufacturing country. The sentiment on this question that has always prevailed in England was voiced by Lord Brougham in 1816, in a remarkable speech relating to the financial and industrial condition of England, in which he recommended to British manufacturers to export and sell their products in this country at a loss, holding that it was well worth while to incur a loss upon first exportations, in order by the glut to stifle those rising manufactories in the United States; stating that after this was done the British manufacturers could put their prices back where they could make a profit that would not only recompense then from their sacrifices made in destroying manufactures.
>
> This advice of this great statesman has been adopted by English manufacturers again and again during the last seventy years. There is scarcely a successful industry which is now amply and fully protected under exiting law that has not felt the crushing effect of that policy under previous inadequate import duties; but in every instance where Congress has given the American producers a duty which would be sufficient to protect and encourage the industry, it has not only been successfully carried on, but has furnished the article to the American consumer at a less price than was exacted by the foreign competitor when he controlled the market.
>
> For more than two generations English manufacturers and English importers have taken almost as lively an interest in our Presidential campaigns as the citizens themselves; and ever since the organization of the Republican party the English government, regardless of the political divisions at home, have been united in their opposition to policy of the Republican party and to its political success. The reason is plain. The Republican party has advocated what Henry Clay so eloquently styled the American policy.

U.S. opposition to free trade, a staple of 19th and early 20th century U.S. foreign policy, metamorphosed itself into unwavering support from 1934 on. With the signing of the Reciprocal Trade Agreements Act of 1934, President Franklin D. Roosevelt signaled the beginning of U.S. free trade. The latter, like in the United Kingdom a century earlier, was founded on industrial supremacy, specifically on electro-magnetic power-based mass production, which like steam power-based mass production, contributed to a manifold reduction in costs and prices, and the birth of American industrial supremacy (Beaudreau 1996,1999), and on the emergence of private networks in the form of U.S. multinational firms.

Membership in the resulting economic networks, as pointed out, is no longer based on geopolitical considerations, but rather, is based in large measure on favorable terms of trade. If welfare-improving trading opportunities exist, then exchange will likely occur. Unlike geopolitical economic networks, purely economic networks are, by design, less stable. Owing to a multiplicity of factors, trade opportunities may be ephemeral, here today, and gone tomorrow. Such uncertainty can exact a heavy toll on both firms and countries. Take the case of firms. Firms having large sunk costs run considerable risks in the presence of uncertain feed-stocks.

As I will argue in Chapter 5, the rise of the vertically-integrated firm was, in part, a response to this risk. High-throughput manufacturing firms (Ford, General Motors, Chrysler) integrated vertically, thus minimizing feedstock risk. Seen from another angle, the vertically-integrated multinational firm can be seen as an attempt to re-introduce the stability of geo-political (governance) networks in a free-trade environment.

Today, the presence—and, indeed, dominance—of the vertically-integrated multinational firm as the principal form (institution) of international exchange is further proof of the ubiquity of networks as the dominant trading institution. Large-scale spontaneous exchange, as described by political economists from David Ricardo to Paul Krugman, is an empirically vacuous concept, having little relevance in past, present, and, undoubtedly, future international trade. This raises a number of questions, not the least of which is why? Why does conventional trade theory rest on the assumption of spontaneous exchange among sovereign nationals of different countries, when historically, such trade has never existed—and judging from current trends, will never exist?

The book is organized as follows. Chapter 2 examines networks from different angles, with an eye to identifying similarities across disciplines. I begin with the role of networks in multi-cellular evolution. This is followed by a look at neurological mappings of social networks. Evolutionary anthropologists believe that the ability to network is intimately tied to cortical area of the brain. The bigger the forebrain, the argument goes, the greater the ability to network. This is then followed by a detailed chronology of the rise of great trading empires and civilizations. Chapter 3 presents an evolutionary model of networks, one that derives networks from first principles—that is, in lieu of assuming their existence. Chapter 4 presents a model of what archaeologically and historically constitutes the most important form of gains from trade, namely between raw materials and transformation (value added). This is referred to as vertical trade—as opposed to horizontal trade. The archaeological and historical record shows that the bulk of trade has, in one form or another, involved raw materials and transformation. A good example today is Japan's foreign trade, where finished goods are exported and raw materials are imported. Chapter 5 sets out to test the resulting model of vertical network trade. Among the issues examined are the factor content of vertical trade, as well as the corresponding dynamics. Chapter 6 examines trade policy from a network perspective. It begins by identifying the relevant policy parameters, and proceeds to examine a number of case studies. Chapter 7 discusses the many implications (theoretical and ideological) of the network approach to trade for international economics, not to mention, international studies in general.

2

Trade and Networks

During the first 3,000 years of civilization, armies and empires reigned. One armed state after another would emerge to dominate, and sometimes destroy their neighbors. From Africa to Asia, from the Bronze Age to the Iron Age, kings led their armies in an endless struggle for power, sometimes winning a brief ascendancy for a century of more.

2.1 Introduction

Networks abound in nature, whether it be in the realm of multi-cellular organisms or social interaction. Common to all is exchange, whether it be goods and services, genes, energy, etcetera, is the presence of a well-defined structure. One could argue that networks and network structure are universals, crossing disciplines and time. That is, networks as a form of organization confer certain advantages to members regardless of the trade involved. It is with this notion in mind that I examine, in this chapter, the myriad aspects of networks, beginning with the networks that are multi-cellular organisms. This is followed by a discussion of the role of the human neo-cortex in social networks, with particular emphasis on information transmission, storage and retrieval. This then sets the stage for a reexamination of the rise of large-scale specialization and exchange, a development that defines the Neolithic era.

2.2 Definitions

One of the greatest difficulties facing those working in the field of social networks, of which trade networks are an example, is the very definition of a network. While we know that trade networks exist—and have existed—there are few formal definitions—other than mathematical and engineering ones. What constitutes a trade network? What are the necessary (sufficient) conditions? Are countries trade networks, do trade networks exist within countries? Are multinational firms trade networks? If so, why?

I begin with definitions of networks. Dictionaries define networks as follows:

> A large system consisting of many similar parts that are connected together to allow movement or communication between or along the parts or between the parts and a control center. (Cambridge Dictionary)

> 1: a fabric or structure of cords or wires that cross at regular intervals and are knotted or secured at the crossings. 2: a system of lines or channels resembling a network. 3: a) an interconnected or interrelated chain, group, or system a network of hotels b): a system of computers, terminals, and databases connected by communications lines. 4: a) group of radio or television stations linked by wire or radio relay b): a radio or television company that produces programs for broadcast over such a network. (Merriam-Webster WWW Dictionary)

Common to each is the notion of physical relationship or connectedness—of fabrics, channels, computers, terminals, etcetera. I shall refer to such networks as physical networks. The problem, however, is that trade (social and economic) networks are not physical entities—that is, do not have a physical representation.

This led me to other network forms or network representations (physical), notably, to what neuroscientists refer to as neural networks, which, by definition, are based on the information transmission, storage and retrieval capacities of the brain, specifically of the neo-cortex. The relevant structure is similar to, in many ways, other physical networks; however, there is no physical structure other than the human brain, and the information stored therein. For example, one's network of friends is nothing more than information on a set of individuals that is stored in one's cortex. This information consists of what they look like, how they behave, and one's feelings towards them. One's social network consists of the same information, but with a wider, more diverse set of feelings (good, bad, indifferent).

Clearly, neural networks are the basis of social networks, and, as such, are at the very root of the social sciences and humanities. That is, social scientists are interested in the formation and evolution of neural networks, which, as pointed out, are the basis of social activity. It is my view that neural networks are more complex than physical networks, the latter having the distinct advantage of being more concrete.[1]

Understanding why or how our neo-cortex evolved over time making us the most social of primates is, in my view, an infinitely more challenging task than modeling computer networks. In this chapter, trade (neural) networks are examined over time, beginning with pre-history, the underlying idea being that the historical record may provide helpful clues to the questions at hand (i.e. those pertaining to the origins of neural trade networks). The starting point is paleoneurology, specifically, the study of the evolution of the brain, and its role in social activity (networking and trade). It is argued that the neo-cortex (neo-pallium), is an information processing device that evolved largely in response to the exigencies of trade. Networking, it is argued, is a dominant evolutionary strategy, conferring important advantages on the members. Larger brains, with their greater ability to store and process information, were selected for in a Darwinian sense.

2.3 Single-versus Multi-Cell Organisms

It is commonly accepted that life on earth began roughly four-billion years ago, consisting, for the most part, of single-celled organisms. Six-hundred and eighty million years ago, there was what Matt Ridley refers to as a "new world order," marked by the invention of "bigger, multicellular creatures." It is suspected that this resulted from the pooling of, or combining of, single-cell genes. Put differently, from the networking of single-cell organisms. According to Matt Ridley:

> There is, however, a conceptual difficulty about trying to identify the earliest forms of life. These days, it is impossible for most creatures to acquire genes except from both parents, but that may not always have been so. Even today, bacteria can acquire genes from other bacteria merely by ingesting them. There might once have been widespread trade, even burglary, of genes. In the deep past chromosomes were probably numerous and short, containing just one gene each, which could be lost or gained quite easily. If this was so, Carle Woese points out, the organism was not yet an enduring entity. It was a temporary team of genes. The genes that ended up in all of us may therefore have come from lots of different 'species' of creature, and it is futile to try to sort them into different lineages. We are descended not from one ancestral Luca, but from the whole community of genetic organisms. (Ridley 2000, 20)

Such "genetic networking," however, gave way in time to "vertical inheritance," the process whereby evolution is governed by gene mutation. The result, according to microbiologist Carl Woese, is a classification of life forms based on three domains, bacteria, archaea, and eucarya. The important point, as far as networks and networking are concerned, is the absence of a common universal ancestor. The universal ancestor is not a discrete entity, but rather, a diverse community of cells that survives and evolved as a biological unit.

2.3.1 Social Behavior

Once "horizontal inheritance" gave way to "vertical inheritance," networks and networking became extra-genetic, that is, operating outside the realm of genetics. Networks and networking, in this case, increased the genetic fitness of a species relative to all other species. The better a species was at networking, the greater were its chances of survival Thus was born what I refer to as social networking, and, consequently, social networks. The historical record, both ancient and modern, is replete with example of network dominance. Species that cooperated, establishing networks, did better than those that did not. Our species considered by most to be the most dominant of all species, is a case in point.

Thus, at the most elemental level of life, networking played a pivotal role, providing the genetic wherewithal for the emergence of multicellular organisms. Conceptually, the resulting multicellular organisms (moistly eucarya) were undoubtedly genetically fitter than the source organisms (archea), or alternatively, were able to occupy an ecological niche until then vacant.

2.4 The Cerebral Cortex, Trade and Networks

It is generally accepted that what distinguishes our species, Homo sapiens-sapiens from all other mammals—and indeed, reptiles— is our capacity for social behavior—socialization, to put it differently. Socialization, however, is nothing more than trade activity, trade being broadly defined. It therefore follows that trade, more specifically, our heightened ability to trade (social, economic, political) is what makes us what we are. The medium of trade, in both real and representational (virtual) space, is language. Without language, trade would be impossible. Conversely, without trade, language would be superfluous. This, of course, parallels merchant trade and money.

Without money, large-scale merchant trade would be near impossible, and without trade, money would be superfluous. This raises a number of questions, the most important of which is why? Why do we trade more than any other species? Why is trade (all forms) so much greater in Homo sapiens-sapiens than in our closest genetic relatives (species)? Why is it that lower primates, other mammals and reptiles do not trade? After all, gains from trade and specialization abound in the natural world.

The answers to these questions, I argue, are important for a number of reasons, not the least of which is the question at hand, namely why we as a species trade in well-defined, well-structured networks. As our species has not, over the course of the last 300,000 years, undergone any significant genotypical and phenotypical changes, it stands to reasons that answers to these questions should provide important insights into trade patterns today, and well into the future—that is, until our species undergoes significant modifications.

2.4.1 The Cerebral Cortex and Information Storage and Retrieval

It is generally accepted that, anatomically speaking, what distinguishes our species from all other primates, is our big brain, specifically, our big cerebral cortex, which, on average, is 1,006,525 mm^3. Table 2.1, taken from Dunbar (1992), presents data on neo-cortex volume, hind brain volume, total brain volume (neo-cortex and hind brain), along with body mass, neo-cortex ratio as well as Jersion's extra cortical neurons index, for 38 primate species. Comparing Homo sapiens-sapiens to gorillas, we find that while the latter have a relatively large neo-cortex (341,000mm^3), when compared to other primates, it is literally dwarfed by that of Homo sapiens-sapiens (1,006,525 mm^3). The neo-cortex ratio (neo-cortex volume/(brain volume-neo-cortex volume) for the former is 2.65, and 4.10 for the latter. Jerison's extra-cortical neurons index is 3.58 for gorillas and 4.10 for Homo sapiens-sapiens.

In light of this (socialization and cortex size in Homo sapiens-sapiens), it could be reasonably argued that our relatively large cortex has something to do with our heightened socialization and trade activity. That is, our cortex (neo-pallium), in combination with our limbic system (paleo-pallium) and our so-called reptilian brain (archi-pallium) (McLean 1982), is somehow responsible for our extensive socialization and trade. If one considers the fact that trade is an information-intensive activity (transmission, storage and retrieval), then it follows that trade would be an increasing function of cortical development (size and specialization). Information requirements include (*i*) the ability to consciously identify needs, (*ii*) the ability to identity and locate potential traders (*iii*) the ability to read the intentions of potential traders, (*iv*) the ability to communicate (transmit) these needs, (*v*) the ability to evaluate the goods and services being traded, and (*vi*) ability to identify the probability of loss—including loss of life. Species with smaller cortexes, it therefore follows, have a lower capacity to store and process information, resulting in lower overall trade (socialization and economic).

Table 2.1
Neocortex Size in Primates

Genus	Body Mass	N	H	Total	C_R	N_C
Cebus	3,100	46,429	13,088	66,939	2.36	1.19
Saimiri	660	15,541	4,938	22,572	2.21	0.55
Macaca	7,800	63,482	16,817	87,896	2.6	1.27
Cercocebus	7,900	68,733	20,555	97,603	2.38	1.53
Papio	25,000	140,142	35,971	190,957	2.76	1.99
Ceropthecus	4,850	47,550	13,272	67,035	2.44	1.02
Miopithecus	1,200	26,427	7,610	377,766	2.33	
Erythrocebus	7,800	77,144	18,398	103,167	2.96	
Pygathrix	7,500	48,763	16,341	72,530	2.05	
Nasalis	14,000	62,685	21,924	92,787	1.75	
Procolobus	7,000	50,906	15,933	73,818	2.22	
Hylobates	5,700	65,800	21,504	97,505	2.08	1.37
Gorilla	105,000	341,444	100,480	470,359	2.65	3.58
Pan	46,000	291,592	68,611	382,103	3.22	3.26
Homo	65,000	1006,525	188,449	1,251,847	4.10	8.52

Source: Dunbar (1992).

2.4.2 Cause and Effect

This raises the obvious question of which came first, the chicken (trade) or the egg (cortex)? From an evolutionary point of view, it could be argued that the cortex evolved in response to the exigencies of genetic fitness-increasing trade activity—often times proxied by group size (socialization). That is, selection pressures favoring increased trade activity would have contributed to the evolution of larger cortexes. If trade and socialization increased genetic fitness, then it stands to reason that the species would have selected for larger-cortexes. That is, members of a species with larger cortexes would have had greater access to resources, including food and females, etcetera. This process would have continued over time, giving rise to new species (via speciation), one with a larger cortex, and an even greater capacity for socialization.

Table 2.2
Genetic Fitness-Increasing Networking Activities

Defense
Hunting
Tool Making
Religion
Agriculture
Irrigation

Table 2.2 lists possible genetic fitness-increasing networking activities, including defense, hunting, tool-making, religion, agriculture, and irrigation (van Schaik 1983; Wrangham 1987; Dunbar 1988). Each can be viewed as a form of public good.[2] In each, the probability of success is increasing in network size, as measured by the size of the group. The point that I would like to make here is that either of these (or related) activities could have favored the emergence of social networks, and, consequently, the evolution of large cortexes. Robin Dunbar, in an article entitled "Neo-cortex size as a constraint on group size in primates," published in the *Journal of Human Evolution*, favors the "defense against predators" hypothesis.

> The strong correlation between terrestriality, large cortex size, large body size and large groups suggests that predation risk is the more likely of these alternatives, since it is difficult to see why large groups should be needed to defend the food sources of terrestrial species but not those of arboreal species. (Dunbar 1992, 490)

2.4.3 The Neanderthal Enigma

One of the mysteries of paleoanthropology is the fate of Homo sapiens neanderthalensis, believed to be our closest relative, and, according to some, our direct ancestor. Why is it that, after thousands of years of cohabitation with Cro-magnons, they suddenly disappeared some 30,000 years ago, leaving no trace? What happened? After all, anatomically, they differed little.

James Shreeve, in *The Neanderthal Enigma—Solving the Mystery of Modern Human Origins*, points to Cro-magnons differential ability to form alliances (networks), conferring a decisive advantage in trade, specifically the exchange of raw materials needed to fabricate tools, and in defense. Alliances, he notes, are Pareto increasing, especially in times of crisis (e.g. climatic change).

According to Shreeve:

> Let's begin with the rocks that move. In Bulgaria, a thousand miles east of Dolni Vestonice, there is a cave called Bacho Kiro. Excavated by a team led by Polish archeologist Janusz Kozlowski, it is famous for containing the earliest known Aurignacian assemblages, and thus the first, formal evidence of upper Paleolithic culture, 43,000 years old. The distinctive, blade-based Aurignacian artifacts are utterly different from the Mousterian hand tools found below then in the cave's deposits, suggesting that they were the handiwork of people who arrived in the area from somewhere else. We do not know where they came from, but we can trace the movement of their rocks. While the Mousterian tools in the case were hacked out of unwieldy volcanic basalt found in the immediate vicinity, most of the Aurignacian tools in Bacho Kiro wer made of high-quality flint imported from the outcrops anywhere from fifty to seventy-five miles from the mouth of the cave. (Shreeve 1995, 289)

He goes on to explain:

> Normally, stone is sedentary: the only time rocks move is when people carry them, or trade them through a chain of exchanges that covers the same distance. The same goes for shells. Molliscs from the Black Sea moved to the central Russian Plain; others found in Gravettian sites in Germany have been traced to species native to the Mediterranean, four hundred and thirty miles to the south as the crow flies. Pierced marine shells from both the Atlantic and the Mediterranean coasts adorned the necks of Cro-Magnon hunter-gatherers in the Perigord, two or three hundred miles from the sea. They were also making beads out of talc. There is no talc in the Perigord. The nearest outcrops are in the Pyrenees, far to the South. (Shreeve 1995, 298)

In the Upper Paleolithic—as opposed to the Lower Middle Paleolithic—the stone used for tool making was imported over long distances, pointing unequivocally to the presence of extensive trade networks (alliances).

> Rocks traveled across the landscape during the Middle Paleolithic too, but rarely so far and never so much. In the later Middle Paleolithic record of Central Europe, as French archeologist Jehanne Feblot-Augustins has shown, tools can be found over one hundred miles from the source of the raw material used to make them. But such peripatetic stone was the exception, not the rule; 99 percent of the stone tools in any given site were made on materials found within twelve miles. In the equivalent Middle Stone Age in southern Africa, the percentage of imported flint in some Howieson's Poort sites was close to half, but the distance seldom exceeded twenty-five miles. In short, long-dis-

tance procurement of raw materials did not seem to be part of the repeated pattern of human behavior until the beginning of the Upper Paleolithic. And it is the repeated pattern that reflects what people are really up to. If raw material was moving more, then so, it would appear, were the people. (Shreeve 1995, 299)

Alliances, Shreeve goes on to argue, act as an insurance policy, increasing the probability of survival in times of crisis.

Apparently, the Cro-Magnon hunter-gatherers who followed them enjoyed another alternative: They could make friends. Not just friends within the group or among close neighboring groups, but friends in distant places encountered on long treks; friends who until encountered, might have been total strangers. If you are a hunter-gatherer in a marginal environment, these are the kind of allies you need. They are your insurance policy. In the event of local catastrophe, being part of an alliance is the only way you can be assured of a friendly welcome to the resources of another group over the mountain or across the plain. Ten years later, a drought might give your people a chance to return the factor. (Shreeve 1995, 299)

As this example illustrates unequivocally, genetic fitness is increasing in the ability to network, so to speak. While there can be little doubt that Neanderthals possessed the ability to network, what is clear is that, relative to Cro-Magnons, it was limited and limiting. By forming larger, more complex networks, Cro-Magnons were able to oust their closest cousins, the Neanderthals, from a shared ecological niche, and occupy it alone.

2.4.4 Cerebralization and Evolutionary Psychology

Put differently, as is commonly believed in evolutionary psychology and biology, structure reflects function, and not vice-versa. According to evolutionary psychologists Leda Cosmides and John Tooby:

The function of the brain is to generate behavior that is contingent upon information from an organism's environment. It is, therefore, an information-processing device. Neuroscientists study the physical structure of such devices, and cognitive psychologists study the information-processing programs realized by that structure. There is, however, another level of explanation—a functional level. In evolved systems, form follows function. The physical structure is there because it embodies a set of programs; the programs are there because they solved a particular problem in the past. This functional level of explanation is essential for understanding how natural selection designs organisms. (Cosmides and Tooby 1998, 12)

The view that our cortex evolved in response to the exigencies of trade (socialization) finds support in evolutionary psychology, specifically from research which shows that the human mind "contains a large collection of functionally specialized computational devices analogous to expert systems in artificial intelligence or, more loosely, to the specialized application programs people use on their personal computers. Just as personal computers now commonly come factory pre-installed with such specialized programs as a word-processor, spreadsheet, calendar, drawing programs, etc., so too the human mind appears to have, as part of its species-typical design, a rich and heterogeneous set of evolved cognitive programs (also called by other terms such as modules or adapted specializations) (Bergstrom *et al* 1998, 3)."

Evolutionary psychologists posit the existence of a number of such cognitive programs, including cooperation, grammar acquisition, face recognition and interpretation, aggressive threats, in-groups and coalitions, contagion, hazard avoidance, incest avoidance, learning about the biological world, inferring the contents of others' minds, etcetera. What is important to note, as far as we are concerned, is that most of these programs (mechanisms) are trade-related, trade being broadly defined.

2.4.5 Implications for the Study of Trade

Understanding neural processes, specifically, their origins and purposes, I argue, is essential to understanding behavior. For example, to understand trade and socialization, one must understand the way in which our evolved brain processes trade-related information. Examples of the latter include information on potential trading partners (reputation), price, quality, quantity, and the associated risks. As information is both necessary and costly, it follows that trade (socialization) is more likely to occur in well-defined networks. Extra-network (spontaneous) trade is, as such, highly unlikely. This, I argue, has important implications for the study of trade activity in general, and world trade in particular.

For example, we know for a fact that social trading is predominantly carried out in well-defined and well-structured networks. Spontaneous, unstructured trade is the proverbial exception that only confirms this rule. The reason is simple, namely that spontaneous trade is a costly activity, one fraught with danger (e.g. risks and perils), owing, in large measure, to the presence of incomplete information. This, I argue, explains why we, as a species, have traded, trade, and will continue to trade in well-defined networks. In fact, one could argue that we as a species do not choose between spontaneous trade and non-spontaneous trade, but rather between no trade (autarky) and non-spontaneous trade. Put differently, the only choice we as a species actually make, is between autarky and network trade. A good example of this is mate selection, where we invest substantial resources in information collection, and networking. This is not surprising given that the institution of monogamous marriage constitutes a network in which a good part of a spouse's lifelong trading (socialization) will take place.

2.4.6 Axioms and Theorems of Cerebralization and Trade

As a guide to understanding the evolution of trade and socialization, I present the following axioms. First, there is the axiom of cerebralization and trade-related information storage and processing. According to this axiom, the level of trade-related information storage and processing is, in general, increasing in the size of the cerebral cortex. The bigger is the latter, the greater is a species' ability to store and process trade-related information. Second, there is the axiom of trade-related information storage and processing and trade (socialization), according to which trade is increasing in a species ability to store and process trade-related information. Combining these, one obtains a basic trade theorem, namely that trade is increasing in cerebralization. Species with large cortexes are, as such, more likely to trade, the cortex being the "trade central processing unit."

2.4.7 Evidence from Non-Human Primates

In an article entitled "Neo-cortex size as a constraint on group size in primates," evolutionary anthropologist Robin Dunbar, using data on neo-cortex volume, group size, and a number of behavioral ecological variables in 38 primate genera, found that group size was positively correlated to neo-cortex volume. The latter was measured in a number of ways, including (1) absolute neo-cortex volume, (2) relative neo-cortex volume (measured as the residual of neo-cortex volume regressed on either body mass or the rest of the brain), and (3) neo-cortex ratio (calculated as the ratio of neo-cortex volume to the volume of either the rest of the brain or the hindbrain).

Dunbar (1992) plotted mean group size among the 38 genera studied against the neo-cortex ratio (3). The greater is the latter, the greater is mean group size.

In other words, the greater is the capacity to process trade-related information, the greater is the size of the group or network. Dunbar, using regression analysis, found that the neo-cortex ratio (3) best explained the data.

From a trade and networks point of view, these results suggest that the neo-cortex, in its capacity of information storage and processing device, is a necessary condition for trade, as measured here by mean group size. Further, they suggest that while homo sapiens-sapiens with his large neo-cortex is the most social of primates, mean group size is nonetheless finite. In other words, there is an optimal size of the group, which Dunbar estimates at roughly 150 members.

2.5 Large-Scale Specialization and Exchange

2.5.1 Proto-Empires: Sumer and Assyria

As these examples illustrate, the ability to network conferred and confers an evolutionary advantage, namely that of increasing genetic fitness. This is consistent with the principles of basic institutional economics, as described by John R. Commons in his 1931 *American Economic Review* paper:

> If we endeavor to find a universal circumstance, common to all behavior known as institutional, we may define an institution as collective action in control, liberation and expansion of individual action. Collective action ranges all the way from unorganized custom to the many organized going concerns, such as the family, the corporation, the trade association, the trade union, the reserve system, the state. The principle common to all of them is greater or less control, liberation and expansion of individual action by collective action.

It stands to reason, however, that at any particular point in time in evolutionary time, a specie's information storage and retrieval capacities (neo-cortex) would impose a limit (constraint) on network size. Put differently, that a specie's capacity to process trade-related information (size of neo-cortex) is limited places an upper limit on the size of the relevant trade network. According to Leonard Dudley:

> Stripped down to its bare essentials, a community may be viewed as a group of individuals who acquire, store and exchange information; that is, a community is an information network. The value of group membership to each individual then depends on the usefulness of the information that he obtains as a result of interacting with his neighbors. Only if the value of what he gains is greater than what he could obtain on his own outside the community is social membership desirable. (Dudley 1991, 38)

In the absence of evolutionary selection for bigger-brained individuals, capable of storing even greater amounts of trade-related information, trade networks (social groupings, societies) should remain relatively constant over time. Evolutionary anthropologist Robin Dunbar estimates maximum group size at 150 for Homo sapiens-sapiens.

As it turns out, however, a number of innovations, beginning in the upper Paleolithic era, served to relax this constraint. One such innovation was the advent of mnemonics or symbols—in short, the development of culture. Membership in a tribe, clan, or network, could now be established by say, a type of sword, knife, or, even, a figurine. A good example of this is the Franks, whose identity was tied to a specific type of weapon. The important point, as far as the current discussion is concerned, is that such mnemonic devices increased greatly the potential size of the alliance or network.

> Whatever triggered the burst of new humanity, it amplified the need and the opportunity for more sophisticated political communication. As alliances began to coalesce on the landscape, they introduced the possibility that there were people out there, beyond one's circle of relatives and familiars, who might not be something inherently, viciously, lethally hostile. But not every stranger would be friendly. Artifacts thus began to take on style when social interaction was gripped by a new, energizing quality: ambiguity.... The emergence of style in artifact design is only one feature of the Upper Paleolithic. But once utilitarian objects like spear points carry social messages, would it take any great leap of imagination or technical know how to create artifacts that had no utilitarian function, whose sole adaptive purpose was to carry social information.... Not every aspect of the Upper Paleolithic can be swept into a single, grand explanation, but it seems to me that an immensely important step occurred when people crossed the barriers of mutual distrust and connected across landscapes, in the process recruiting mere materials to express those connections, to carry information and ideas. After that, the world ceased to be taken at face value and came alive with metaphor, symbol, and layered subtleties of inference and possibility. (Shreeve 1995, 304)

The information content—and, indeed, possibilities—of such mnemonic devices was, however, limited, specifically to membership, and rank. Detailed trade-related information could not be stored nor retrieved. However, some 30,000 years later, the information storage and retrieval constraint referred to above was further relaxed with the appearance of writing and record keeping. Writing and record keeping increased markedly a society's ability to store and retrieve information. One could go as far as to argue that the advent of writing and record keeping can be seen as an extension of the human brain's information storage and retrieval capacities. Now, trade-related information for hundreds, even thousands, of individuals could be kept.

Table 2.3
Trade-Related Information Storage and Processing Devices

Cerebral Cortex
Culture
Writing and Record Keeping

The results were felt immediately. With the advent of writing and record keeping came the first large-scale trade networks, also known as empires. The Sumerian Empire and the Egyptian Empire are cases in point.

Chronologically speaking, writing and record keeping on the one hand, and large-scale trade networks on the other hand, appear to be contemporaneous. This raises a number of questions. For example, what factor or factors prompted the development of writing and record-keeping? What would have prompted uncharacteristically large numbers of human beings to want to organize themselves in a network and trade? By inference, we know that the cause was most certainly trade related.

Larger numbers (i.e. agglomeration), one could argue, conferred some advantage, until then either unknown or unexploited, on both the Sumerians and Egyptians. There are a number of possibilities, including religion, defense, and public works, each being a form of public good. Consider first the case of religion. Suppose that the late fourth and early third millennia witnessed a heightened awareness of spirituality, marked by an increased demand for religious ceremonies and, the emergence of competing priests and temples. In such a setting, some priests and temples may have experienced large increases in membership, making it difficult, if not impossible, to keep track of all members, and their offerings. Record keeping, it therefore follows, may have had its origins in large-scale, broadly-based religion (temples).

A similar story could be told in the case of defense, namely, the development of large-scale armies staffed by professional soldiers. In such a case, there would be obvious size (scale) related advantages, which would, in the long-run, favor the development of large-scale armies. Again, writing and record keeping would be required to monitor membership in the trade network, and the payment for defense services. Lastly, there is the possibility that writing and record keeping came about in response to a need to organize large-scale public works. Again, the idea is similar, namely that a system of records was required without which finance could not be arranged.

Personally, I favor the first hypothesis, for a number of reasons, not the least of which is the fact that ancient cities were literally built around the temple (e.g. ziggurats). The temple—and, in some cases, palace—stood at the center of the city and, consequently, at the center of all economic activity (socialization). What differentiates the agglomerations (social networks) of Mesopotamia and Egypt from all others is the presence of a massive—for the period—temple. As most church leaders know perfectly well, a moderate-to-small size church (temple) requires some form of writing and record keeping to establish membership and, most importantly, keep track of offerings. Second, there is the question of ability, specifically, the ability to devise a written language—that is, invent a written record-keeping device. This amounts to asking which of the two groups, priests or warriors, appears most likely to devise a written language? Here, the odds would seem to favor priests over warriors, for obvious reasons.

Regardless of their origins, writing and record keeping prompted a paradigm shift in Homo sapiens-sapiens' ability to network, the result of which were the first cities, and the first empires. Common to both was trade, on a local level (cities) and on an international level (empires). Further, once established, the institutions (writing and record-keeping) of the networks lent themselves to numerous other applications, including such things as large-scale public works. According to Leonard Dudley, the invention of writing, by increasing the amount of information available, permitted the construction of large-scale public works.

> The evidence from Sumer suggests that the invention of writing permitted a population increase by raising the total area of land that could be cultivated. Writing reduced the degree of asymmetry in available information between administrators and those who worked for them, enabling more effective monitoring of subordinates. The new information system therefore raised the number of individuals whose activities could be effectively coordinated, permitting the construction of large-scale public works projects such as extended irrigation canal networks. As water became available at considerable distances from the river's edges, more land could be brought under cultivation. (Dudley 1991, 32)

2.5.2 Network Ladders

Clearly, the advent of writing and record keeping altered forever the nature and scope of social networks. Never again would the human brain, specifically, the human memory, place an upper limit on the size of the relevant trading network (society). Similarly, never again would a shared culture impose an upper limit on the size of the relevant trading network. Theoretically, at least, there was no information-based limit to the size of the resulting trade network. In practice, however, there were limits, limits imposed by either the very nature of the relevant public goods, or by nature. For example, in ancient Sumer and Assyria, there would have been an upper limit on the number of individuals worshipping at any given temple. Transportation costs and the very fact that temples could not accommodate more than a fixed number of worshippers are examples. Table 2.4 presents what I refer to as a network ladder, showing the different levels of agglomeration and, consequently, of trade in the presence of writing and record-keeping (non-cortex-based information storage). In order, there is the city-state, the nation-state and, lastly, the empire. The information storage-based requirements increase with each phase.

Table 2.4
Network Ladders

Phase I: City State
Phase II: Nation State
Phase III: Empire

2.6 Mesopotamia and Egypt

Being the birthplace of writing and record keeping, it should come as no surprise that Mesopotamia, a land saddled between the Tigres and Euphrates rivers in what is today Iraq, was the cradle of large-scale trade networks, commonly referred to as civilization, or "life in the city." In each city, life (trade) revolved around the temple (ziggurat). Physically, the latter, without exception, was located at the very center of each city. Among the cities of Mesopotamia were Akkad, Ur, Nineva, and Uruk. Table 2.5 presents the three eras of Sumerian trade network development, along with a brief description of each. The first phase, the City-State, describes Sumeria prior to the reign of Sargon I of Akkad, that is, prior to the unification of city-states. This phase is characterized by the presence of independent city-states, each physically built around a temple. The provision of public goods, I maintain, was the primary source of organized trade, which is not to say, however, that it was the only source. Spontaneous, small-scale, tangential trade may have occurred.

In every civilization the network of social interaction is articulated within established channels that are coordinated in a characteristic and unique manner. For Mesopotamia, one such pattern of integration found its most direct expression in the city. This pattern maintained its effectiveness through three millennia of history. In order to study and to analyze it adequately, its composite nature has to be recognized as an essential feature and the components have to be investigated, first separately and then in their relationship to one another.

Let us distinguish two essential components: first, the community of persons of equal status bound together by a consciousness of belonging, realized by directing their communal affairs by means of an assembly, in which, under a presiding officer, some measure of consensus was reached as it was the case in the rich and quasi-independent cities of Babylonia; second, an organization of persons entirely different in structure and temperament from the community just mentioned, whose center and raison d'être was either the temple or the palace, either the household of the deity or that of the king. Both were closed-circuit organizations in which goods and services were channeled into a circulation system and where the entire personnel was integrated in a hierarchic order. (Oppenheim 1964, 95)

Table 2.5
The Sumerian Trade and Network Ladder

Phase I: *City State*

-Presence of a pure public good (e.g. god, army, irrigation).
-Temple-Palace as provider of public good.
-Trade is local, involving public good.
-Barter is prevalent transactions technology, and palace-temple officials oversee trading.
-Treaties govern extra-city-state trade.

Phase II: *Nation-State*

-Presence of a pan-city-state (national) public good.
-City-state government defers to national government.
-Trade is national.

Phase III: *Empire*

-Same as Nation-State.
-Presence of a pan-city-state (empire) public good.
-City-state government defers to national (empire) government.
-Trade is inter-empire (international).

In general, trade involved food and raw materials, in return for public goods (defense, religion). Taxation (temple dues) in kind, or later in money, was the chief form of exchange. Extra-city state trade by citizens was not permitted. However, there is evidence that such trade was carried out by temple and palace officials on a ritualized and reciprocal basis (i.e. among priests and rulers).

According to Leo Oppenheim, two types of foreign trade were present in Mesopotamia, namely the export of what I refer to as industrial goods, and the carrying trade.

> On principle, two types of foreign trade, as well as intercity trade, have to be distinguished. First is the export of industrial goods, which in Mesopotamia means, as we have seem, textiles produced by serfs in the self-contained organizations of the temple or palace to create the means of exchange needed for importing metal, stone, lumber, spices and perfumes. The second is a carrying trade between foreign cities, trading outposts, and barbarian tribes who lacked the prestige, the political power, and the initiative necessary to engage in trade relations on the basis of treaties. Both types of trade are attested around the Persian Gulf and Asia Minor before the Dark Age as well as along the Euphrates route into the Mediterranean littoral before and after that period. (Oppenheim 1964, 91)

This phase gave way, in the reign of Sargon I of Akkad, to both the Nation-State phase and, ultimately, the Empire phase. A number of factors, I argue, contributed to this, not the least of which was the fact that writing and record keeping made large-scale agglomeration organizationally possible. However, growth and the need for scarce raw materials, I argue, are what prompted Sargon I of Akkad to unify Sumeria into the equivalent of a Nation-State. It must be pointed out that the very nature of public goods (non-convex) facilitated the task enormously. Common defense systems and common belief systems (religions) were, as a result, shared by all Sumerians. Citizenship in the larger agglomeration, as in the smaller city-states, could be closely monitored by means of written records (birth records, censuses, etcetera).

As a result, certain Sumerian city-states (examples) transformed raw materials into finished goods, while others provided raw materials. Trade, from very early on, was predominately industrial in nature, involving raw materials for value added.

It is important to point out that these network-based gains from trade transcended time, and, in the case of Sumeria, the various dynasties and dynastic rulers. The trade networks that first emerged in early Mesopotamia lasted over 2,000 years, and, more importantly, laid the foundations for civilization as we know it today. As I shall attempt to show in this chapter, and indeed, throughout this book, the Sumerian trade network characterized by the presence of government (public goods), and the exchange of raw materials for value added, differs little from all other trade networks since. In fact, one could go as far as to argue that, production technology aside, the network technology found in Imperial France and Great Britain, and more recently, in the United States, differs little from that of ancient Sumeria. Further evidence of this comes by way of Egypt, where, almost simultaneously, large-scale trade networks (societies) emerged. Chronologically, it was in the Third Millennium that the first pharaoh, Menes, united Egypt, until then a land of independent city-states on the banks of the Nile river.

> In the Late Predynastic period (3,400 to 3,100 BC) two independent kingdoms grew up. Both were similar in that they consisted of small independent districts, each of which had a main town, a local god, and a chieftain. The northern kingdom in the Delta has its capital at Pe whose protective deity was the cobra-goddess; the southern kingdom in Upper Egypt has its capital at Nekheb, near Hierkonpolis, under the case of the vulture goddess Nekhbet. Little is known of the rulers of these kingdoms, but fragments of a mace-head found at Hierkonpolis belonging to a king-Scorpion are decorated with scenes showing his victory over enemies and his development of the irrigation of land. It is likely that Scorpion paved the way for Narmer's later resounding success in unifying the country. The history of dynastic Egypt was born with the conquest of the north by a southern king, Narmer-Menes, who then proceeded to make himself king of a united Egypt. (David 1988, 13)

Three successive empires (Ancient, Middle, and New) followed, each consisting of a series of dynasties (Memphis, Licht, and Thebes, respectively). This was followed by a series of empires, known as Amenophis I. Thoutmosis I, and Thoutmosis III). The borders of these empires extended from Napata to the south, to Byblos in Syria to the North.

As was the case in Sumeria, empire trade consisted largely of raw materials for value added, the latter in the form of finished goods (see Table 2.6). Among the imports were timber, arsenic, copper, tin, lapus lazuli, obsidian, and medicinal plants; among those exported were yarns, fine linens, glass bottles, vases, embroidered work, potter's wheels, weaver's looms, pulleys, and valves. What is noteworthy is the fact that most manufactures were produced in government-owned (or sponsored) factories.

As pointed out above, trade networks are information and record-keeping intensive. Before large-scale networks can emerge, a society has to somehow solve the information and record keeping problem referred to earlier. A single human

brain could not, at this point in time, store and retrieve the vast amounts of information needed to trade on a large scale. As it turns out, the Egyptians had solved
this problem, by developing a form of writing known as hieroglyphics, and a
form of paper, known as papyrus. Both, I argue, were necessary conditions in the
ascent of Egyptian civilization.

2.7 The Roman Empire

In the second and third Millennium, Sumeria and Egypt laid down the blueprint
of modern-day civilization. Government, writing, codified law, and trade, were
its cornerstones. In the second and third Millennium, what is present-day Rome
was little more than a village. One thousand years later, it would become the center of one of the greatest empires (trade networks) in the history of mankind,
namely the Roman empire, organized around a city-state. In this section, I examine the rise of the Roman empire, focusing on the corresponding networks
(social, political and economic). It will be argued that as was the case in Sumeria
and Egypt, the Roman empire grew in stages, beginning with the city-state, and
culminating with the empire. In each stage, trade was dominated by the palace-
temple. While much is known of Rome from 753 BC on, little is known of
ancient Rome, that is, Rome before Augustus. What is known, however, is that
early Rome was one of a number of city-states of ancient Latium. Each was organized around the temple-palace, as had been the case in ancient Sumeria and
Egypt. Similarly, each was relatively self-sufficient. Unfortunately, little is known
of this period. Questions abound. For example, why had the member city-states
of Latium declared war on each other?

Table 2.6
Trade Patterns in Ancient Egypt

Imports

Timber (from Syria and Lebanon)
Arsenic and Copper (from Cyprus)
Tin (from Asia and Europe)
Lapus Lazuli (from Afghanistan)
Obsidian (from Abyssinia)
Medicinal Plants (from Africa and Near East)

Exports

Yarns
Fine Linens
Glass Bottles
Vases
Embroidered Work
Paper
Potter's Wheels
Weaver's Looms
Pullies
Valves

While historians have, until now, attributed such conflicts to personalities, specifically, the personalities of various leaders, the analysis presented above suggests other causes. As had been the case in the past (ancient Sumeria, Egypt), and would be the case in the future (Holy Roman Empire, French and British colonial empires), the underlying reason could conceivably have been trade related, specifically to the gains from trade. As city-states increased in size, shortages appeared. In some cases, palace/temple officials could, by way of inter-city-state trade, ease these shortages. However, when negotiation failed, armed combat ensued, the end result of which was conquest and geographic aggrandizement for the victors in this case, the Romans.[3]

Conquest, as argued earlier, was preferred for a number of reasons. First, the conquerors gained access to scarce resources, resulting in important gains from trade. Second, by extending existing palace-temple (government-religion) to a larger base (population), more rents could be extracted—at least, potentially. Third, the conquered gained access to resources, and, quite possibly, a more advanced culture (government-religion).[4] By advanced, it should be understood, larger networks and intra-network specialization.

2.7.1 History

The history of the rise of the Roman empire, from early Latium, to the fourth century AD, is, in essence, the history of three successive large-scale trade networks, each building on the previous ones. The initial trade network is the city-state of Rome, where trade was local in scope, and involved, in large measure, the exchange of palace-temple services. This was followed by Rome as the center of Latium and modern-day Italy. The corresponding trade network was more expansive, and, more importantly, was joined by a system of roads that was revolutionary. As the saying goes, "all roads lead to Rome," which is not surprising given the nature of trade networks

As the empire grew, so did the city of Rome, making it increasingly dependent on outlying regions for its primary commodities, including food, wood, cotton, and other raw materials. As had been the case in Sumeria and Egypt, network trade consisted of raw materials and energy (foodstuffs and slaves) from the outlying regions for finished goods and government from the core, in this case, Rome. Included in government are technology and culture, broadly defined.

As is well known, slave labor was the principal source of energy for Roman society, driving its manufacturing and public works. As the slaves themselves were not a source of energy per se, but rather converted the energy stored in proteins and carbohydrates into work, its follows that the ultimate source of energy in the Roman empire was the food (grains) it imported from its colonies. In short, the Roman empire, like all other empires before and after, was founded on wealth creation through network trade. Energy and raw materials were imported from the periphery, with organization (technology, administration) being provided by the core, in this case Rome. The periphery exported raw materials and energy, and imported finished goods and Roman public goods (technology, culture). The core imported raw materials and energy and exported what was essentially knowledge (culture, technology, administration).

The resulting large-scale trade network view of the ancient economy (Sumeria to Rome) is consistent with that of A. H. M. Jones and Sir Moses Findlay of Cambridge University, known as the "new orthodoxy."

> The new orthodoxy stresses the cellular self-sufficiency of the ancient economy; each farm, each district, each region grew and made nearly all that it needed. The main basis of wealth was agriculture. The vast majority of the population in most areas of the ancient world was primarily occupied with growing food. To be sure, there were exceptions (such as classical Athens and the city of Rome), but they were exceptions and should be treated as such.

> Most small towns were the residence of local large-landowners, centers of government and religious cult; they also produced market-places for the exchange of local produce and a convenient location for local craftsmen making goods pre-dominantly for local consumption. The scale of inter-regional trade was very small. (Garnsey *et al* 1983, *xi*)

It is also consistent with the historical record which shows that the bulk of international (inter-city-state, inter-nation-state) trade was carried out by governments (palace-temple) and executed by government officials (temple-palace officials). Spontaneous international trade was discouraged, and, in many cases, forbidden. In many instances, taxes were levied on foreign imports. Moreover, foreigners, most often, foreign traders, were ostracized from civil society, and, in most cases, obliged to take up residence in ghettos (foreign quarters).

The treatment of everything foreign (goods and individuals) in the ancient economy can be attributed in large measure to the nature of civil society, namely being based on membership in a trading network, itself founded on a public good (temple, palace, defense). Imports acted as a drain on fiat money, and, more importantly, constituted a leak in terms of government revenue. Trades involving foreigners reduced government revenue, as compared to trades involving citizens. I shall return to this in the next chapter.

2.8 Free-Trade Imperialism

In addition to providing its numerous possessions (colonies) with its technology and culture, the Roman empire provided them, as the Sumerians had done with the Assyrians, with the knowledge of the structure and workings of large-scale trade networks, specifically, the knowledge of the corresponding gains from trade. With the coming of the Renaissance, and, more importantly, improvements in sailing technology, came a new era of empire (trade network) building, one based in Western Europe, more specifically in seafaring nations like France, Spain, Portugal, etcetera.

The story of each, as it turns out, strangely resembles that of Rome, with a few nuances. Specifically, neither France, Spain or Portugal developed new technologies as had the Romans. In short, all three were nation-state trade networks built on the foundations laid by Rome. This then raises the obvious question of the gains from trade. In the absence of new technologies, how could an empire be assembled.

As it turns out, this was not entirely true, for while they had no new technologies per se, they did have one important advantage, namely, sailing technology.

In short, Roman civilization had not reached much the world's population, owing to the lack of a suitable communication technology. Innovations in transportation in the 14th, 15th and 16th century changed this, with the result that new opportunities presented themselves, and were seized by former Roman colonies such as France, Spain, Portugal, and, to a lesser extent England, Holland, etcetera.

Each proceeded to amass a trade empire where most of the exchange was either conducted and executed by palace-temple officials, or by agents of the palace-temple. In little time, the world was literally carved up among European nation-states. Within the resulting trade networks, raw materials and energy were traded against finished goods and, for lack of a better word, civilization (Roman), by which it should be understood, elaborate, large-scale well-organized trade networks.

It need be pointed out, however, that while the French, Spanish and Portuguese were responsible for increasing the level of world trade, the world economy in this period was, for the most part, predominantly agricultural. That is, most agents were self-sufficient farmers. Manufacturing was limited, as it had been in ancient Sumeria and Rome. Like the French, Spanish and Portuguese, the Anglo-Saxons of what is now England, being a seafaring nation, had amassed an extensive trade network (empire), with London, an ancient Roman town, as its center. However, while the history of the British empire until the 19th century reads like that of its European rivals, the 19th century marks the beginning of a new type (specie) of trade network, one based less on organization, specifically, on the export of civilization, and one based more on pure commercial exchange. The underlying cause of this change: the steam engine. The steam engine, I argue, changed fundamentally, the nature of exchange in European trade networks (empires). Until the 19th century, the gains from trade, as far as the periphery was concerned, derived from what I choose to call "civilization," that is social trade networks (religion, government, technology). Colonies, until then autarkic for the most part, were literally plugged into a trade network. Raw materials were exported, and civilization and perhaps some finished goods, were imported.

It goes without saying that, to some local notables (in the colonies), the gains from trade would have appeared to have been skewed in favor of the core. The views proffered by the fathers of the American revolution are examples of such views.

The steam engine, I argue, changed all this. First, as Adam Smith argued, the nature and cause of the wealth of nations no longer derived from empire-based rent-seeking activities, but rather from the transformation of raw materials—in short, manufacturing (Smith 1776, 4). While limited in scope throughout much of the history of civilization owing to the energy constraint, the advent of the steam engine, by replacing animate by inanimate power, pushed back the energy constraint, providing a seemingly unlimited source of growth and wealth (Beaudreau 1999, 56). Suddenly, the value of the empire as a rent-seeking institution plummeted. Colonies became less important for the tax revenue they could generate than for their raw materials, or, put differently, their ability to provide the necessary feed stocks for British industry. This, I argue, prompted a number of changes in British foreign policy, including the abandonment of the British empire and the adoption of imperial preference, which marked the birth of free-trade.

> Halevy described Ricardo as the theorist of 'the great English manufacturers, who dreamt of making the economic conquest of the world.' The weapon which the would-be conquerors intended to employ was an international free trade, justified by the doctrine of comparative advantage; the form of this projected economic dominance was to be a trading system established upon England's leading position in industrial production....The view that a freer trade would facilitate the perpetuation of England's industrial dominance was foreshadowed, in a mid-eighteenth-century debate, by Josiah Tucker, a mercantilist, who had become convinced that free-trade was in the British national interest. Tucker's arguments studded the parliamentary speeches in the discussions of Pitt's trade proposals in the eighties. We can follow the development of these ideas in the writings of James Mill, Robert Torrens (whose vision of trade-empire in 1815 was virtually an 'ideal-type' of free-trade mercantilism), David Ricardo, and Edward Gibbon Wakefield, among others. That this substantially mercantilist goal of making England the Workshop of the World, a goal largely set by the economists, was widely accepted, is apparent in surveying the parliamentary debates which led to the abolition of the corn laws, in the course of which Joseph Hume, and finally Sir Robert Peel made themselves its leading spokesmen. (Semmel 1970, 9)

Britain no longer had to govern its former colonies to enrich itself; all it had to do was control the resource (i.e. copper mine, cotton field). According to Bernard Semmel:

> One Whig, speaking before the House of Commons during the Corn Law debate of 1846, described free trade as the beneficent 'principle' by which foreign nations would become valuable Colonies to us, without imposing on us the responsibility of governing them. (Semmel 1970, 8)

Foreign ownership, as it turned out, proved to be superior as a means of wealth creation to colonization. This, I argue, would forever change the nature of trade networks. Hitherto, trade networks would be built around private wealth-generating networks. That is not to say that public institutions (palace-temple) would no longer play a role in trade, but rather that, their role changed. Specifically, heretofore, they would be subordinated to the wishes of private networks, from which their livelihood (tax revenue) would now depend.

The Bank of England in conjunction with the City of London, the army, and the navy played pivotal roles in the creation and maintenance of the British industrial trade network, described by Bernard Semmel as a form of "Free Trade Imperialism." It has been argued that the Bank of England and the City of London, by channeling capital out of the country, were instrumental in keeping the value of the pound low, thus stimulating British manufacturing exports, and, in the process, maintaining the industrial trade network. Further, it set up branches abroad, providing credit to foreigners wanting to do business with the U.K., and acting as agents for British merchants abroad.

In short, the trade network was no longer political in its structure (i.e. empires), but rather, industrial. The center (core) provided a market for raw materials, and, more importantly, provided the institutions of trade, making extra-network trade difficult, if not impossible.

Perhaps the best way to understand Great Britain in the 19th century is by way of analogy. What pushed Great Britain to repeal the "British Empire" and adopt "imperial preference," or "free-trade" was its belief, as firmly held as that of imperial Rome, in its technology. The steam engine-based reduction in the cost of manufacturing finished goods, like Roman architecture, Roman engineering, and Roman culture, would, in a matter of time, lead to world dominance. As Rome once ruled the world, so too would Great Britain, by virtue of its superior technology. And, for a century, it did.

Add to this the fact that lost tariff revenue would be more than made up by tax revenue from British transnational trading companies.

2.9 The United States of America

My interest in the United States as an example of trade networks stems from its past, first as a colony, providing feed stocks to Great Britain, and, in the 20th century, as the dominant manufacturing nation, importing feed stocks from abroad, and exporting finished goods. Like the European mercantile empires (France, Portugal, Spain, Britain), it went from being colonized to colonizing, albeit in a somewhat different way. I shall argue that the United States, following in the footsteps of Great Britain, established a trade network based on industry, not government.

As was the case in Ancient Sumeria, Egypt, and Rome, the rise of the U.S. trade network (empire) was achieved in a number of stages, beginning with the city-state phase, which dates from the founding of the 13 colonies, each an independent state. This was followed by the nation-state phase which began with the American Revolution and the founding of the United States of America. Apart from military considerations (i.e. the desire on the part of Britain to reclaim its former colonies), it could be argued that economic (read: wealth) considerations were foremost in the founding of the union (13 states).[5] In short, the founding fathers sought to create a union the purpose of which was to promote the commonwealth—not the common good, or the common happiness. As outlined by Thomas Jefferson in 1789, trade within the federation (internal trade) would be favored over foreign trade (external trade). All barriers to trade between states were abolished. Later, the Interstate Commerce Commission was established to oversee trade. Throughout most of the 19th century, U.S. territorial expansion occurred in disputed lands, mostly west of the Mississippi. As it turned out, there was little need to go abroad (off-shore). Food was abundant, as were the various feed-stocks for industry, the latter being localized in the Northeast (The industrial heartland stretching from Pennsylvania to Maine).

This, however, changed with the advent of a new energy-based technology, one that would increase radically, the United States' ability to transform feed-stocks, namely electric power. The development of the induction motor by Nikola Tesla and George Westinghouse, ushered in the "second industrial revolution," increasing productivity and doubling growth rates. Rapid growth led to feedstock shortages. In little time, U.S. firms began investing abroad, especially in resource sector. The U.S. vertical multinational firm was born.

The important point here is the nature of the third phase (empire phase), namely, as being non-political. Unlike Sumeria, Egypt, Rome, France, Spain, etcetera, the United States did not colonize outright the various sources of raw materials, but rather, took the necessary steps to control them, specifically via foreign ownership. This contrasts with the British experience in the late 19th century, where, despite being avowed free-traders, continued to colonize foreign lands.

As was the case with Great Britain in the 19th century, the nature of the trade was industrial. The United States imported raw materials and energy, and exported value added (finished products), respecting the archaic pattern in trade networks found in ancient Sumeria, namely of resources for value added (trans-formation), or ultimately, resources for knowledge. Examples of the raw materials imported include wood, wood fiber, and iron ore from Canada.[6]

2.10 The Role of Government in Trade Networks

As I have attempted to show, trade networks, both internal and external, have been many and varied throughout history, from early Sumeria to the modern day United States, with its emphasis on multinational firms. While inter-network trade was virtually absent among 18th century mercantile nations, it is common-place today. Take, for example, Canada which trades with the United States and Japan, Europe and Africa. International trade stood at $5.167 trillion, up 107 percent over 1987. Developed economy trade in 1996 stood at $3.514 trillion, up 112 percent over 1987. Developing economy trade in 1996 stood at $1.460 trillion, up 168 percent over 1987. Most of this trade, roughly 70 percent, is car-ried out by multinational firms, which, as I pointed out earlier, are examples of networks. In this section, I examine the role of government in trade networks. It is argued that the role of government has undergone a number of changes over time. Specifically, for over five millennia, government constituted the driving force behind network creation and maintenance. This, however, changed in the mid-19th century with the repeal of the Corn Laws in Great Britain by Sir Rob-ert Peel, and the enactment of the most-favored nation principle—in short, the beginning of the free trade ideal.

Theoretically, at least, trade would be free of government, that is, free of taxes (including import duties) and free of interference. Merchants from far and wide would trade among themselves, their rights being protected, in a reciprocal fash-ion, by statutory law (common and civil law). Trade would, as such, be free—free of government.

In practice, however, trade was never free of government. As a number of writ-ers have pointed out, the doctrine of free trade, as espoused by the likes of Mill, Ricardo, Torrens, etcetera, was aimed, first and foremost, at dismantling mercan-tilism, and replacing it with institutions and a trading empire that were more responsive to the needs of the manufacturing interests of the nation. The British government did not withdraw from the commercial affairs of the nation. Evi-dence of this is found in the its continued involvement in commerce and com-mercial matters after the repeal of the Corn Laws. The Opium Wars in China are a case in point. Wanting to curb the devastating effects of the opium trade, China attempted to close its ports to British merchants. War ensued, a war that was one-sided, being dominated by the British. In 1842, the Chinese were forced to agree to an ignominious peace under the Treaty of Nanking.

The treaty imposed on the Chinese was weighted entirely to the British side. Its first and fundamental demand was for British "extraterritoriality"; all British citizens would be subjected to British, not Chinese, law if they committed any crime on Chinese soil. The British would no longer have to pay tribute to the imperial administration in order to trade with China, and they gained five open ports for British trade: Canton, Shanghai, Foochow, Ningpo, and Amoy. No restrictions were placed on British trade, and, as a consequence, opium trade more than doubled in the three decades following the Treaty of Nanking. The treaty also established England as the "most favored nation" trading with China; this clause granted to Britain any trading rights granted to other countries. Two years later, China, against its will, signed similar treaties with France and the United States.

It is fair to say that British foreign trade in the late 19th century had little in common with the free trade ideal as described by political economists of the day. By the mid-20th century, the bulk of world trade was not conducted in free markets, but rather, was carried out within vertically-integrated multinational firms (MNFs), whose basic fundamental rights were, again, protected by statutory law. The visible hand of MNFs regulates the bulk of international trade, to the extent that, in general, international markets for raw materials are inexistant. Up to 95 percent of raw materials are traded outside of organized markets (through vertically-integrated firms, contracts, etcetera).

Theoretically, at least, national governments (Great Britain and the United States) were no longer a party to international (inter-network) trade. Conceptually, the latter was be conducted under the auspices of complete markets operating in a well-developed international legal framework. The historical record, however, fails to confirm the presence of idealized free trade. The United States government, like that of Great Britain, has, via its various departments, intervened, and continues to intervene in international trade, diplomatically and militarily. The Gulf War in 1991 is a case in point. Sensing its access to cheap middle-eastern oil threatened, the U.S. government, in conjunction with Great Britain and France, expelled Saddam Hussein from Kuwait. Using a series of well-worn euphemisms such as "strategic interests," the U.S. government has, over the course of the 20th century, intervened diplomatically and militarily throughout the world to protect its privately-held industrial trade network. In this regard, it is no different from the imperial armies of Sumer, Egypt, Rome and Spain.

For the sake of discussion, I identify three forms (levels) of government involvement in trade networks: (1) Imperialism; (2) Free Trade; and (3) Partnership.

2.11 Stylized Facts Regarding Trade Networks

What is clear from the historical record is the overwhelming evidence in favor of network trade over arms-length, spontaneous market trade. The case of the 19th century Chinese concession cities is an excellent example. Instead of trading with local Chinese merchants, France, England, Germany, Italy, Russia, and other imperial powers, set up mini-colonies (concessions), side-by-side in port cities such as Tianjin, Shanghai, Nanking, known as concession cities.

Throughout history, inter-network trade was rare, often times the exception, and far from the rule. In most cases, the trade network served the center's interests, specifically providing raw materials and energy, the latter in the form of slaves (animate, muscular energy). Networks underwent changes. Countries or geographic regions were added, and others were dropped, New France (Quebec) being a good example.

2.12 Trade and Networks: Cause and Effect

Perhaps the most fundamental question about trade networks is that of causality. More to the point, does trade precede or proceed the creation of a network, or conversely, does the creation of a network precede or proceed trade? Another way of framing this question is as follows. Are trade networks the formalization—institutionalization—of spontaneous exchange, or are they a precondition for exchange—that is sequentially prior to? It is perhaps worthwhile here to recall that by trade, it should be understood large-scale, recurrent exchange, and not small-scale, one-shot exchange.

The historical record appears to be non-equivocal—networks precede trade. There are no known cases of trade preceding networks—that is, no known cases of spontaneous trade leading to the creation of a network. From the fourth millennia on, trade has, almost without exception, been conducted in well-defined networks. In fact, as was shown earlier, extra-network trade was discouraged outright.

This leads me to the tentative conclusion that networks are a necessary condition for trade, and, more importantly, chronologically precede trade.

2.13 Conclusions

By way of a conclusion, I would like to raise two points, points which I believe, are essential to understanding network trade, and, by implication, trade in general. The first is ubiquitous presence of government. Throughout history, trade has been conducted under well-defined geopolitical entities, be they empires, networks, countries, etcetera. Put differently, spontaneous international trade, the type found in all international trade theory texts, has been the exception, not the rule. The second point pertains to the very nature of network trade, namely what I refer to as industrial, by which is meant that trade is vertical, not horizontal. Why has trade, almost without exception, been vertical in nature, and not horizontal, as argued in trade theory? Raw materials (commodities) have been—and continue to be—traded for value added (transformation). Trade networks, one could argue, impede efficiency and, consequently, welfare. The relevant question then is, why have they, and do they continue to exist?

3

The Theory of Network Trade

The first life on earth was atomistic and individual. Increasingly, since then, it has coagulated. It has become a team game, not a contest of loners. By 3.5 billion years ago there were bacteria five-millionths of a meter long and run by a thousand genes. Even then there was probably teamwork. Today some bacteria swarm together to build 'fruiting bodies' to disperse their spores. Some blue-green algae—simple bacteria-like life forms—form colonies, with even the rudiments of the division of labour between cells. By 1.6 billion years ago, there were complex cells a million times heavier than bacteria and run by teams of 10,000 genes or more: the protozoa. By 500 million years ago there were complex bodies of animals comprising a billion cells; the largest animal on the planet was a trilobite—and anthropod the size of a mouse. Ever since then the biggest bodies have been getting bigger and bigger.

—Matt Ridley, *The Origins of Virtue.*

3.1 Introduction

If nothing else, the evidence presented in Chapter 2 makes it abundantly clear that civilization in its many incarnations is synonymous with highly-developed networks. Defining moments in the "ascent of man" have involved, in one form or another, networks, whether they involve cells, individuals, regions, or countries. Cromagnons' triumph over Neanderthals, paleoanthropologists now posit, owed to their superior ability to form networks—to structure their social relations. One could go as far as to infer causality, specifically from networks to complexity and civilization. Put differently, that networks and networking are dominant strategies. For example, structured trade dominates spontaneous trade. Military alliances dominate "each man for himself"-type strategies.

41

This chapter examines the underlying rationale behind the creation of large-scale trade networks, paying particular attention to the question of structure. Why and how were these networks formed? Were they spontaneous in nature, responding to gains from trade, or were they the result of a need on the part of individuals to coordinate their actions? In the former, the role of the network is restricted to trade in private goods, while in the latter, it encompasses trade in private goods as well as trade in public goods. The latter implies, by definition, the existence of some form of collective choice mechanism. At stake here is the underlying nature of large-scale networks, namely, are they spontaneous pairing of individuals exploiting gains from trade in what, in essence, are private goods, or are they structured agglomerations of individuals trading public—and private—goods?

The chapter proceeds as follows. First, it will be shown, using simple game theory, that spontaneous trade, as defined earlier, is all but impossible. In other words, large-scale trade networks in which private goods are traded cannot occur spontaneously. In other words, left to themselves, autarkic private agents will not spontaneously specialize and trade.[1] Formally, the Nash equilibrium to the corresponding specialize and trade game is the status quo, namely no specialization and no trade.

Next, I demonstrate that among the available mechanisms to resolve the relevant prisoner's dilemma is public choice (government), which, in turn, requires (1) the presence of some political neural network (public choice), and (2) the existence of some public good (e.g. religion, defense, irrigation). In short, the joint occurrence of a political network and a public good is a necessary condition for the emergence of specialization and trade. Also, it will be shown that the nature of the resulting trade is such that it will be exclusionary. That is, it will be confined to the political network from which it arose. Trade outside the network (political and economic) will be discouraged, if not restricted altogether.

3.2 The Literature

Recently, a considerable work has been carried out in economics on the theory of networks. That this is so comes as somewhat of a surprise, given the overriding intellectual and political ideological context in which it emerged. Much as classical political economy was a reaction to mecantilism and empires (networks), the neo-liberal revolution of the 1980's and 1990's can be seen as a reaction to 20th century mercantilism in the form of Keynesianism. The focus of analysis in both cases was the atomistic individual, devoid of any trade-coordinating institutions, of any mention of networks and/or the dynamics of networks.

Yet despite the ideological odds, a significant literature emerged, one that shows much promise. What then prompted an interest in networks? As it turns out, interest in networks was largely prompted by a series of empirical regularities, particularly with regard to industrial structure and labor-market behavior. Avner Greif (1993) and James Rauch and Alessandra Casella (1998) examined how transnational networks of traders can overcome informal barriers to international trade, such as a weak international legal system and lack of information regarding trading opportunities. Steven Durlauf (1993) demonstrated that network interactions between firms in technologically-related industries can generate multiple equilibria for the aggregate growth of the economy. That it has taken the profession this long to examine such phenomena through the prism of networks is somewhat surprising, given the long history of highly-integrated (vertically and horizontally) firms. See, for example, Sobel (1972) and Chandler (1977).

Others have examined the role of networks in trading systems in general. This is a particularly interesting development given the current intellectual and political idealogical context. Rachel Kranton (1996) examined how anonymous markets and networks can form alternative means of exchange and how the growth of one may undermine the functioning of the other. Raja Kali (1999) argued that the existence of a network has a negative effect on the functioning of the anonymous market in an unreliable legal environment because it absorbs honest individuals and thereby raises the density of dishonest individuals engaged in anonymous market exchange. Gérard Weisbuch, Alan Kirman, and Dorothea Herreiner (2000) demonstrated that the underlying network relationships help to explain the pattern of transactions in the wholesale fish market in Marseille. Robert Feenstra, Tzu-Han Yang, and Gary Hamilton (1999) found that differences in business group networks across South Korea, Taiwan, and Japan are reflected in differences in the quality and variety of the products they export.

Theoretical work on networks has, over the past few years, exploded. Beginning with Robert Aumann and Richard Myerson (1989), theorists have studied how links and coalitions are formed between players (Ellison 1993). More recent contributions have focused on modeling behavior within the network itself, the idea being that agents choose links based on the nature of the expected exchange (strategy) and, correspondingly, the payoff.

While a welcome development in a literature that has, owing to its ideological origins, denied the presence of networks, this body of work has a number of shortcomings, notably with regard to networks themselves. First, there is the underlying approach to modelling networks, notably as emerging in what is otherwise an atomistic, market-based environment. In other words, the starting point is a set of self-sustaining, atomistic individuals who decide whether to establish links.

This view, I maintain, is orthogonal with the role of networks in human history. We as a species did not network because we are human; rather, we are human because we networked. Hundreds of thousands of years ago, our species developed network tools such as a large forebrain (cortex) owing to the advantages conferred upon the species by networking. Being human, it therefore follows, implies networking. From an evolutionary point of view, we have invested and continue to invest in a large forebrain, for the advantages it confers on us as a species. Moreover, our networks are highly complex, consisting of networking tools (memory, language, writing, money, dispute-resolution mechanisms), none of which are referred to in the literature. As such, networking is not a choice, but a way of life. The networks we establish are intertemporal, often lasting a life time. Few are the networks that result from one-shot games.

How then does the literature referred to earlier fit into the grander scheme of things? In essence, it can be seen as addressing a subset of a larger problem, namely, the propensity to network. Using simple trading situations in which networking is modeled exogenously in the form of a constraint (costly links), it examines network formation and stability (Jackson 2003). In this regard, it has more in common with James Buchanan's theory of clubs than with human networks.

In this chapter, an attempt will be made to derive exchange (read: social) networks from evolutionary principles. The chosen approach is both historical and analytical. The archaeological, biological, historical and theoretical evidence presented in Chapter 2 will serve to guide the discussion, and hopefully provide clues in our attempt at an empirically-consistent model of the origins and workings of social exchange networks.

3.3 Definitions of Networks

The economic literature on networks, like the mathematical and engineering literature, defines networks in terms of nodes and edges. This raises a number of questions, not the least of which is structure. Practically speaking, what is a social network. Clearly, it has little bearing to either a computer network, or a telephone network. When agents pay the cost of a linkage, what exactly do they receive in return? Unfortunately, the literature is poorly developed when it comes to such questions, which is surprising given the stakes. If one cannot define either the network, nor the cost of a linkage, then the resulting work has little empirical, not to mention practical, value.

Sociologists have attempted to move away from the mathematical and physical definitions of networks, preferring "actors" to nodes, and "social ties" to edges (links). According to Davern (1997):

> The fundamental components of a network are nodes and connections. In order to develop a network metaphor, sociology has replaced the nodes with actors and the connections with social ties or bonds. Thus, a social network consists of a series of direct and indirect ties from one actor to a collection of others, whether the central actor is an individual person or an aggregation of individuals (e.g., a formal organization). A network tie is defined as a relation or social bond between two interacting actors.
>
> The social network image is one way to conceptualize social structure and, therefore, social networks will be used synonymously with social structure throughout this paper. The social network conception of social structure is fundamentally a relation-centered approach. The relations in the structure are the social ties connecting actors. Furthermore, by positing that relations among social actors form a social structure, network analysis rests on a flexible conception of structure. The flexibility comes from the fact that ties are formed and/or broken the social structure changes. Thus social networks are flexible and dynamic because of the frequency of tie formation and dissolution.
>
> The four basic components of social networks are as follows: (1) the structural component (2), the resource component, (3) the normative component, and (4) the dynamic component. The structural aspect refers to the geometric shape of the actors and ties within a network as well as the strength of the ties. This is the basic building block of network analysis. The resource focus is on the distribution within networks of various characteristics that differentiate among actors within society. Examples of these characteristics are ability, knowledge, ethnicity, estate, gender, and class. The normative aspect of networks refers to the norms and overt rules that influence the behavior of actors within varying networks (e.g., the prevalence of reciprocity, or the level of trust among actors within the network, and the overt rules governing behavior). The normative component is also concerned with the type of tie, which is determined by taking into consideration the social roles connected through a tie (e.g., is the tie between a worker and employer, between friends, between kin, etc.). The dynamic component takes into account the opportunities and constraints for tie formation and the ever evolving network structure. Networks are constantly changing and any network model must describe these

> changes. Together the structural, resource, normative, and dynamic compo-
> nents form the basis of social network research. (Davern 1997, 1)

It is not clear, however, that replacing the words nodes with actors, and link-ages-edges with ties constitutes a step in the right direction. For one, it only begs another question, namely what are ties? How are they created? Are they costly?

This led me to pursue other leads, notably in the field of neurology. While we may not know what a social network is, we know what it is not, notably a physical structure akin to a telephone network. Social networks have no visible structure akin to physical networks. Let us begin with the concept of a link-tie. What exactly is a link-tie, as defined above? As it turns out, neurologically-speaking, a link-tie, as defined by Michael Davern, is information, information that is stored in the frontal cortex (left and right orbitofrontal cortex) on a particular individual. For example, in left and right orbitofrontal cortex, I have information stored on my mother (e.g. intentions, relations, history, etcetera), which I can retrieve. Thus, in her presence, I can trade, knowing what her tastes are, that she does not pose a threat, etcetera. This information and the associated transmission, storage and retrieval structure, all of which are localized in the cortex, is the physical equivalent of social networks. In short, a social network is a neural network, and a neural network is a social network.

This particular finding raises yet another important question in the economic theory of networks, namely, why and how did neural networks arise? As pointed out in Chapter 2, species differ in terms of their cortical capacities. Clearly, what is needed is a theory of evolved neural (cortical) networks. What factors explain inter-species differences in cortical capacity? The answer(s) to this question, I argue, would provide important insights into the role of networks in trade.

As I have attempted to demonstrate, neural networks are means to ends, notably as a way of storing trade-related information. The latter consists of such things as the physical characteristics that necessary to identify a preferred trading partner, as well as personality characteristics (e.g. honesty, intentions, aggression, etcetera).

It is a well accepted fact in evolutionary biology and, consequently, evolutionary neurobiology, that form follows function. Without function, there is no form, owing in large measure to costs. Take for example, the evolved cortex. Our large, evolved cortex is not free, but, rather, comes with a price, specifically with regard to energy. The bigger the brain, the greater the energy requirements. One could, as such, argue that for such a large cortex to develop, it must have conferred an advantage on the species.

This brings us to the next question, notably, what was (were) this (these) advantage(s)? While the answer to this question is beyond the scope of the book we can nonetheless speculate. What we do know is that the advantage was trade related. Among the possibilities are defense, production, and culture, to name a few. Shared defenses could, at least theoretically, contribute to increased genetic survival and fitness, for obvious reasons, as could shared production techniques. Among the latter are group hunting, and tool production.

This brings us to the first proposition regarding networks and trade, notably that networks and public goods are contemporaneous occurrences. Put differently, the presence of a network or the capacity to network (evolved human brain) can be interpreted as evidence of public goods. The more extensive the public good, the larger the network and/or the capacity to network.

What is particularly noteworthy, in so far as this proposition is concerned, is the underlying causality. Genetic fitness-increasing trade activity (public goods) cause networks or the capacity to network, and not the reverse. Remember that networking or the capacity to network (human forebrain) is not costless, biologically speaking.

> In 1941 renowned Cleveland surgeon George Crile suggested that the reason we could afford such an energetically costly brain while other animals could not was that it gave us the ability to produce energy outside the body—for example, by making fire and domesticating animals—and thus more than compensated for its cost. One problem with this hypothesis is that even before our ancestors started to make fire, their brains had become bigger. An increased ability to adapt to new situations and habitats seems to be a more plausible payoff for the high brain-energy expenditure in hominids.

These findings provide new grounds on which to begin constructing an economic theory of networks. Clearly, genetic fitness-increasing trade opportunities underlie networks, or the capacity to network. Species in general, and our species in particular, weigh the costs of investing in networks (via larger frontal cortexes) against expected benefits. Members of the species will then form networks that are exclusive in nature. That is, they will exclude all non-members. Trading among members will be exclusive, and at the expense of trade with non-members. The lower are the costs of networking, and the greater are the expected benefits, the greater the likelihood and scale of networking.

3.4 Exclusive versus Non-Exclusive Exchange Networks

Exchange networks can be either exclusive or non-exclusive. By exclusive, it should be understood that all exchange is confined to the network. As a corollary, non-exclusive networks allow for extra-network exchange. A golf club is an example of a non-exclusive network, whereas a trade empire is an example of an exclusive trade network. The Church of the Latter-Day Saints is another example of an exclusive trade network. Religious cults are, in general, exclusive exchange networks. This raises a number of interesting questions, not the least of which is what determines whether a network will be exclusive or non-exclusive? Why have trade networks (cities, states, countries) been predominantly exclusive trade networks.

The literature offers little by way of answers. Typically, agents are confronted with the choice of belonging or not belonging, to the network under consideration. Theoretically, it would stand to reason that exclusivity would be somehow related to the very existence of the network. That is, outside-of the network trade would somehow undermine the integrity of the network. Otherwise, there would appear to be no reason to impose exclusivity. In what follows, I propose a theory of exclusivity in so far as large, highly specialized, trading networks are concerned. The theory is based on two theorems, namely the first and second spontaneous private market impossibility theorems. Both show the non-existence of trade equilibria, and the need for third-party (read: government) intervention. Government intervention in the form of public expenditure constitutes the defining feature of the corresponding network. As large-scale trade depends on government expenditure, and government expenditure is a public good, large-scale trading networks are exclusive. That is, extra-network trade is not allowed.

3.4.1 Markets as Exclusive Trade Networks

The first spontaneous private market impossibility theorem examines the emergence of markets, defined as the stratification/specialization of individuals according to function, of which I focus on two, namely specialized producers, and specialized traders. Both are necessary conditions for markets (large-scale) to exist. To begin with, I assume that individuals are autarkic. That is, they are able to nourish, clothe and house themselves. The question I ask is simple, namely, in the absence of a third party (coordination), can markets, defined as the presence of specialized producers and traders, emerge spontaneously? Put differently, can specialized traders set up shops (trading posts) and specialized producers provide the wherewithal of trade, namely goods.

Let us ask the counterfactual question, what if no one specializes, and no one wants to trade? Then what? Will markets exist? Suppose that, to begin with, agents are autarkic, but, for some reason, want to specialize and trade. As markets (specialized traders) do not exist, the relevant question becomes, how can they emerge? How can would-be specialized producers convey (signal) their intentions to would-be merchants? Likewise, how can would be specialized traders convey their intentions to would be specialized producers?

This problem can be formalized in terms of what I refer to as a Nash specialization game, involving two subsets of agents, one that decides on whether or not they will become specialized producers, and another that decides on whether or not they will become specialized traders (e.g. merchants).

3.4.2 The First Private Market Trade Impossibility Theorem

Consider the case of n geographically-dispersed agents (Homo sapiens-sapiens), each capable of producing the m goods considered necessary for sustaining life.[2] Put differently, each agent can, using his scarce—limited—energy and organization, produce sufficient quantities of each of these goods. Or, he may decide to specialize and produce a subset of the m goods.

Next, suppose there exists a subset of the n agents, k, whose comparative advantage lies in trading, defined as buying goods with the express purpose of reselling them. That is, they are more adept at setting up trading posts where the m goods are traded (Howitt and Clower 2000), than the other $n - k$ agents.

The Nash specialization game can be modeled as follows. The $n - k$ would-be specialized producing agents will choose to specialize if and only if trading posts exist, that is, if the k would-be specialized trading agents specialize and set up trading posts.[3] The reason is straightforward: without trading posts, autarky dominates specialization. For example, someone producing only salt would, in the absence of trading opportunities (read: trading posts), surely perish from lack of sustenance. Next, consider the would-be specialized trader's problem. For him to specialize (i.e. set up a trading post), it need be the case that some of the $n - k$ agents specialize. Setting up a trading post would, in the absence of merchandize to sell (specialization), be pure folly.

As our would-be specialized agents are assumed to play Nash strategies, it follows that specialization and large-scale (organized) trade are, theoretically, impossible.

Theorem 1

If specialization on the part of the $n - k$ would-be specialized producing agents is a function of specialization on the part of the k would-be specialized trading agents (i.e. potential traders), and specialization on the part of the latter is a function of specialization of the former, then overall specialization and trade cannot emerge, at least not spontaneously.

Proof

The proof is relatively straightforward, and consists of showing the existence of an indeterminacy. Specifically, if specialization on the part of the would-be specialized producers depends on specialization on the part of the would-be merchants, and if specialization on the part of the latter depends on specialization on the part of the former, then the outcome is indeterminate.

It follows that if and only if one of the two groups (would-be producers and would-be traders) is willing to pre-commit to specialization (in either production or trade) without any commitment or pre-commitment on the part of the other group can the possibility of trade arise. If would-be producers commit to specialization, then arbitrage opportunities will exist, thus providing an incentive for the k would-be trading agents to specialize—that is, become specialized traders. Put differently, trade will emerge only if either specialization is present, or markets exist. A good example of this is sexual reproduction. In sexual reproduction as opposed to asexual reproduction, specialization is already present in the form of the anatomically distinct males and females (i.e. mammals). It follows that in this case, trade for the purpose of procreation will—in fact, must—occur.[4]

One could argue that nature, millions of years ago, somehow solved this indeterminacy. Theorem 1 rules out the spontaneous emergence of large-scale exchange-based economies (specialized producers and merchants). It does not, however, preclude trade on a small scale—that is, in the absence of trading institutions. For example, two neighboring autarkic farmers or hunter-gatherers could spontaneously engage in mutually-advantageous bi-lateral trade involving fortuitous surpluses. The point of the matter, however, is that such trade is not "market" trade, involving specialized trading agents (Howitt and Clower 2000). Furthermore, one could argue that while possible, such trade (small-scale) is improbable given the unlikely presence of a basis for trade (i.e. the endowment problem). Put differently, it is highly unlikely that neighbors, living in what are identical physical settings, would have anything to trade. There are exceptions such as the presence of mineral springs, obsidian deposits, etcetera. The problem, as I have shown, is a signaling one. Without actually specializing—at great risk—there is no credible way for would-be producing agents to signal to would-be trading agents their demand for intermediation (markets). One way to get around this problem is via a well-established social-political network (Suk-Young Chwe 2000), allowing for communication and coordination. If agents can communicate and coordinate, then they could, quite conceivably, decide to specialize and exchange. This raises another important question, namely, what could/ would prompt individual autarkic agents to communicate and coordinate?

In this chapter, I consider one possible cause, namely, the emergence of public goods. Consider the case of a pure public good (defense, religion), in the presence of a collective-choice mechanism. The latter consists of a decision mechanism that allows individuals to collectively signal their demand for the public good in question. It can be easily shown that, in such a case, specialization and exchange can emerge. In other words, the presence of public goods is a sufficient condition to resolve the indeterminacy.

Take, for example, the case of religion. Individual agents demand religious services (priest, temple), and agree to pay for these services by way of what is commonly referred to as taxes (user fees). A priest would be chosen from among the congregation, and the remaining members would agree to pay him a salary. In so doing, specialization and exchange, heretofore indeterminate, will have occurred. The important point here is that the political network (collective-choice mechanism) would have "made the market" so-to-speak. That is, given rise to large-scale specialization and exchange. The more public goods (religion, defense, irrigation), the greater the level of specialization and exchange, measured by the level of taxation.

Such a system, while feasible, would be very cumbersome, owing to a number of factors, not the least of which is the level of organization required—especially as the number of agents (i.e. members of the network) increases. The government would need numerous warehouses and a virtual army of civil servants (i.e. royal merchants, royal notaries, royal tax collectors) to oversee exchange activity. Further, price lists would be exhaustive, having no less than $n(n-1)/2$ prices (exchange ratios).

One way to reduce these costs is to introduce a material unit of account, otherwise known as a money ($n + 1th$ good). For example, the government (collective-choice mechanism) could issue a fiat currency, use it to pay for public goods (e.g. religion), and declare it legal tender—in other words, make taxes payable in it. This would reduce the costs of transacting considerably. For one, it would reduce the number of prices to n, n being the number of goods/services. Second, it would reduce the organizational costs. Government officials (royal merchants) would simply purchase goods and services from agents, offering money in return.

It is likely that by monetizing the economy, exchange in general, would increase, as secondary markets would arise, consisting, on the supply side, of agents who do not deal (directly) with royal merchants.[5] That is, individuals who do not deal directly with the government. As taxes are payable in the fiat currency, it stands to reason that these agents, in order to fulfill their civic obligations, would have to somehow trade with agents who, in fact, trade with royal merchants. That is, those who trade goods and services with royal merchants in return for money.

Again, in this case, the government, by way of its purchases, will be responsible for prompting specialization and exchange (secondary)—in short, for making the market. The more the government spends, the higher will be the overall tax liability, and, hence, the higher will be primary and secondary trading. If resources are not fully employed, then it stands to reason that government expenditure will contribute to increasing overall wealth (realized).

3.4.3 Making the Market and Exchange Exclusivity

Given the fundamental indeterminacy described in Theorem 1 in conjunction with the role of government in its resolution, it stands to reason that the resulting trade network would be exclusive. That is, trade is restricted to members of network. Trade by non-members would be akin to free-riding, free-riding on members who collectively contribute to making the market.

This brings us to the second spontaneous private market trade impossibility theorem, which is based, in large part, on the problem of making the market. As has been shown, the government, through its demand for public goods, "creates" or "makes" the market. The more its spends, the higher the overall tax liability, and the greater is the resulting level of economic activity—provided of course that the economy is operating below capacity. This raises another question, namely can private merchants in combination with private producers (i.e. nongovernmental) "make the market?" In other words, can merchants, by unilaterally increasing their purchases of goods and services, "make the market," or, in a growth context, increase the market? I now examine this question.

3.4.5 The Second Private Market Trade Impossibility Theorem

Suppose that, to begin with, there are three types of agents, royal merchants, who carry out the affairs of the state (collective-choice mechanism), private merchants, who buy and sell goods and services from agents, and, lastly, agents who produce, sell and buy goods and services, as well as pay taxes. Further, assume that there exists a credit-issuing bank whose sole purpose is providing credit to merchants (royal and private)—production is assumed to be "in-house," requiring no credit (cottage industry).

In this hypothetical setting, both royal and private merchants are responsible for making the market, the former via the government's demand for public goods, and the latter via its demand for trade credit. Private merchants require trade credit to finance their purchases of goods.

Define c_j as merchant j's demand for credit and c as the aggregate level of credit outstanding. The individual private merchant's problem, it therefore follows, consists of maximizing profits, defined as the difference between his revenue (sales at his shop) and his costs (purchases from producers). Formally, this corresponds to $\pi_j = 1/k[c] - c_j$. For the sake of simplicity, I assume that aggregate sales are divided (apportioned) equally among private merchants. That is, each merchant receives an equal share of c, the aggregate level of outstanding merchant credit.[6]

Now, let us turn to the question at hand, namely whether private merchants and private producers can, in the absence of a third party, spontaneously make the market. To address this question, I model the individual private merchant's problem in terms of a Nash non-cooperative game. That is, private merchants set c_j taking other c_j's as fixed.

The relevant question, it therefore follows, is whether an individual private merchant has an incentive to increase his purchases of goods from private producers and, in the process, increase, c. To ask the question is to answer it. Clearly, the representative private merchant has no private incentives to purchase goods from producers.

Theorem 2

Starting from a no-trade position, the representative private merchant has no incentive to make the market, which, in aggregate, results in a no-trade equilibrium.

Proof

The proof is simple, and consists of showing that for all c_j greater than 0, the representative merchant's profits, *ceteris paribus*, will be negative. Specifically, $\pi_j = 1/k[c_j] - c_j < 0$.

These two theorems highlight the social—as opposed to the private—nature of trade and exchange in a decentralized setting. Characterizing both are various indeterminacies, each associated with what are, in essence, Nash strategies. In games in which players play "I'll go if you go" strategies, the outcome is always the status quo (inertia). Trade requires communication and coordination. Specialization requires markets and markets require specialization. Similarly, individual private merchant's orders for goods from producers are premised on the existence of similar orders on the part of other private merchants. To put it simply, highly organized forms of trade require communication and coordination, or put differently, some form of government.[7]

3.4.6 Spontaneous Private Market Impossibility Theorems

As I have attempted to demonstrate here, the spontaneous emergence of organized private non-exclusive markets is tenuous at best. Indeterminacies and prisoner's dilemmas militate against specialization and market activity as we know it today. This raises the obvious question, namely if spontaneous trade is impossible, then how did specialization and markets—and money—arise? The answer, I argue, can be found in ancient history, specifically, in Mesopotamia, and involves large-scale public goods (e.g. organized religion and defense). The decision to erect massive temples (ziggurats) and to create a caste of individuals (priests) whose task it was to conduct religious ceremonies (services), prompted citizens of the ancient cities of Eridu, Ur, and Uruk, to solve the coordination problem referred to earlier, by imposing specialization and trade, the latter taking the form of taxes in kind. In these cities, religious rite defined membership, or, put differently, citizenship, in a particular urban agglomeration. The point is that large-scale organized trade—and civilization—was the result of government, of a political network that made collective choice possible, without which modern civilization may have never emerged.

The rise of civilization, however, was not without obstacles, some more serious than others. Perhaps the greatest was what I shall refer to as the problem of information, or, simply, the information problem. A prerequisite for public choice is a system of writing and record keeping. While decision making does not forcibly require writing or record keeping, the outcome does. For example, Eriduians could have collectively decided to build a ziggurat (temple) without writing and record keeping. If, however, they decided to finance it by way of a head tax, then writing and record keeping would have been necessary, for obvious reasons, not the least of which is the classic "free-rider problem." At the time, each Eriduian could be made better off by not paying the head tax.

One could argue that the free-rider problem (truthful revelation), in combination with the storage and retrieval limits of the human brain, are what prompted the development by priests of writing and record keeping. The archeological evidence is unequivocal: early Sumerian cuneiform was first used to record what appear to be transactions (trades, exchanges). One could go even further and argue that these records are those of the temple or palace, and pertain to the payment of a head tax. Written records of public accounts were a *sine quo non* of civilization. Take away writing and record keeping, and large-scale agglomerations disappear, ceding their place to smaller agglomerations such as tribes and bands.[8]

3.5 On Man's Fundamental Nature

As the Nash specialization game makes abundantly clear, primates are, by their very nature, autarkic. That is, in the absence of a large cerebral cortex, writing and record keeping (extensions of the former), public goods, and public-choice mechanisms, primates would, like their mammalian cousins, be solitary and autarkic. Civilization, markets and trade, as I have attempted to show here, are the result of public goods and public-choice mechanisms.

It therefore stands to reason that any and all Homo sapiens-sapiens cultures will rest on public goods and public-choice mechanisms, however different, and however varied. Government, defined as a communication and coordination network, is the foundation of civilization, of trade, and of markets. One could go a step further and argue that public goods and public choice mechanisms are the source of all trading, social and economic. Take, for example, Christmas, which, while a religious holiday, is an event that prompts people to trade. Family members who would otherwise not see each other and trade (social and economic), are united, and trade. Professional sports, one could argue, are analogous, in the sense that they prompt social activity (trading) on the part of spectators (present and via the various media).

In short, while primates, as a species, are autarkic by nature, homo sapiens-sapiens have developed cultures that are biased toward trade and social activity.

Regardless of whether culture consists of college football or the opera, or whether members of the society declare themselves against government (e.g. Americans), the fact remains that we, under the threat of the first trade impossibility theorem, require trade-prompting activities.

3.5.1 Domain-Specific Reasoning and the Free-Rider Problem

Evidence that early forms of exchange involved public goods is provided by the findings of social contract theory in evolutionary neuropsychology. Neuropsychologist Lea Cosmides has argued that reasoning processes are domain specific as opposed to domain general. One such reasoning process is what has become known as "cheater detection." Drawing from experimental results involving the Cassava rule (if P-not Q), she found evidence of a cheater-detection algorithm in Homo sapiens-sapiens.

Put differently, we as a species developed domain-specific reasoning, in this case, the ability to detect free-riders. Seen through the prism of evolution, it stands to reason that such domain-specific reasoning was fitness-increasing. That is, it conferred advantages on our species. Homo sapiens-sapiens could, as a result, produce and consume collective goods (public goods) that increased their genetic fitness. An example of this would be a fortified structure that provided members of a specific groupings with defense services. In the next section, it will be argued that civilization and cites as we now understand them were made possible by this form of domain-specific reasoning as both are synonymous with collective consumption.

3.6 Government and Exclusive Trade Networks

In ancient Mesopotamia appeared the first cities (large-scale). At the center of city life were the temple and its priests. In time, the needs of the temple, commodity-wise, led to the development of manufactures, localized around the temple (i.e. in the vicinity of the temple). In most cases, objects of adoration and worship were fashioned out of rare (read: scarce) materials. With the growth of cities, the demand for such materials increased, resulting often times in shortages. This, in turn, resulted in territorial expansion, and the birth of political federations and empires, as was shown in Chapter 2.

At the center of the resulting trade activity was government, without which exchange (large-scale) would have been impossible. Government, by way of its needs (demands), made the primary market. Royal merchants confidently increased expenditure, knowing full well, that they, unlike private merchants, would be able to pay off any of the debts incurred by way of the sovereign's power of taxation.[9]

Private merchants had no such assurances, which, as shown earlier, is the root cause of the first spontaneous private market impossibility theorem. This is not to say that private merchants could not, theoretically, make markets. Take, for example, the second spontaneous private market impossibility theorem. If by chance all private merchants simultaneously increased their demand for credit by ten percent, then overall income would rise by ten percent, resulting in a ten percent increase in overall economic activity. Barring such occurrences, there are no private incentives to make the market.

As political agglomerations (empires) expanded, both through population growth and immigration, the need for resources increased. In time, the needs of the state increased, requiring increasingly more resources, and, consequently, leading to an increase in the volume of trade. The latter was achieved via taxation in kind, which was, in essence, payment for defense services rendered. The same was true of religion. In time, barter—and the corresponding centralized administration—was replaced by fiat money as the relevant exchange technology. To minimize transactions costs, governments issued money, used it in trade, set prices in terms of it, and, most importantly, required that taxes be paid in it.[10] This marked the beginning of legal tender, where, by government decree, government-issued (fiat) money became the exchange medium by the force of law.[11] In recent work, Robert Clower and Peter Howitt derive monetary exchange in a setting characterized by specialized producers and specialized traders—in other words, in the case in which agents have somehow solved the first spontaneous private trade impossibility theorem. Governments made the market via their purchases of goods and services. As taxes had to be paid in fiat money, those not trading with the government (issuer of fiat money) were forced to trade with those who did in order to obtain the wherewithal (i.e. fiat money) to pay their taxes. This marked the birth of monetized private markets. Specialization and trade flourished. Those who had, up until then, been autarkic, specialized, resulting in increased non-governmental trade.

The point of the matter is that governments (collective-choice mechanisms), by imposing trade, were, in large part, responsible for the emergence of specialization, markets and money. In the case of large-scale organized religion, church members were required to pay for religious services by way of recurrent offerings. In barter economies, individual agents took advantage of the coordinating aspects of the religious service to trade surplus goods (that is, after the religious offering was paid). This explains, I believe, why temples were also places of commerce and exchange.[12]

3.6.1 John Law, La Banque Générale, and the Compagnie d'Occident

Few are those throughout history who understood, or appreciated the first and second spontaneous private market impossibility theorems. The institutional basis for civilization in general, and large-scale exchange in particular, has, for millennia, been ignored, its essential role in social and economic exchange over-looked.[13] Yet, as the first spontaneous private market impossibility theorem makes abundantly clear, inertia is, by far, the most likely outcome in "I'll go if you go" games.[14]

Among the few—and first—to appreciate this fundamental aspect of trade was the much maligned French financier John Law, who founded *La Banque Générale*, and *La Compagnie d'Occident*.[15] Law understood that exchange and markets are not spontaneous in nature, and that, in the absence of government, unrealized trading opportunities would abound.

> Domestick Trade depends on the Money. A greater Quantity employes more People that a lesser Quantity. A limited Sum can only set a number of People to Work proportion'd to it, and 'tis with little success Laws are made, for Employing the Poor or Idle in Countries where Money is scarce; good Laws many bring the Money to the full Circulation 'tis capable of, and force it to those Employments that are most profitable to the Country; But no Laws can make it go furder, nore can more People be set to Work, without more Money to circulate so, as to pay the Wages of a greater number.
>
> National Power and Wealth consists in numbers of People, and Magazines of Home and Foreign Goods. These depend on Trade, and Trade depends on Money. So to be Powerful and Wealthy in proportion to other Nations, we should have Money in proportion with them; for the best Laws without Money cannot employ the People, Improve the Product, or advance Manufacture and Trade. (Law 1705, 14)

What is particularly revealing is the way in which Law set out to stimulate the French economy at the request of the duc d'Orléans. Rather then setting up a bank for the purposes of extending credit to private entrepreneurs, he set up a "royal" bank, *La Banque Générale*, which, by royal decree, issued prodigious quantities of notes, notes that were used to finance government expenditure. In short, the duc d'Orléans' behavior was no different than all other monarchs, namely spending to stimulate trade, or, put differently, "make the market."

What differentiated Law's scheme from previous ones was its corporate nature. Put differently, the finances of the state, France, would be privatized, so to speak. Law's company was granted the ability to issue notes, in return for a share of the profits. Peter Garber described Law's rationale as follows:

> Law (1705) sketched a monetary theory in an environment of unemployed resources. In such an environment, he argued, and emission of paper currency would expand real commerce permanently, thereby increasing the demand for the new currency sufficiently to preclude pressure on prices. To finance a great economic project, an entrepreneur needed only the power to create claims which served as a means of payment. Once financed, the project would profit sufficiently from the employment of previously wasted resources to justify the public's faith in its liabilities. (Garber 1990, 41)

The key, argued Law, was the government's ability to create money (fiat money). In a world of unrealized trading opportunities, an inflow of new government expenditure, financed by a new issuance of fiat money, would stimulate trade, and, via the resulting taxes, allow the government to balance its books, so to speak.

Governments, he argued, were not particularly adept at overseeing the creation of markets. Expenditure was oftentimes erratic, being determined by the vagaries of war. Clearly, what was needed was a "market-making" branch of the government, one that would overcome the inertia referred to earlier, and "make markets." To this end, he proposed to "privatize" the creation of markets, creation and the collection of taxes in the form of a joint-stock company. The latter would have the right to issue fiat currency and collect taxes. It would "remit" an annual dividend to the government which would be used for government expenditure. Growth, erratic until then, would become more regular as a result, with the issuing of new fiat money every year. Unused or under-used resources would be called into action. The *Compagnie d'Occident*, it therefore follows, should be understood as a reaction to (*i*) the spontaneous private market impossibility theorems, and (*ii*) the erratic nature of government expenditure.

3.6.2 Foreign Trade and the Nation-State

Throughout the ancient economy, foreign (non-exclusive) trade was discouraged, to the point of being forbidden in many countries. While, at first, this might appear irrational, especially in light of non-negligible gains from trade, it is, nonetheless, consistent with the theory of network trade presented here. Spontaneous trade, as I have showed, is impossible, both in a non-monetized and monetized economy. Governments create markets by way of (1) public expenditure (2) issuing fiat money and (3) requiring taxes to paid in it (i.e. the legal tender). Free extra-network trade, I argue, poses a problem—if not two or more. First, if network member countries import goods from a third country, then this acts as a leakage on aggregate (network) income—and (fiat) money. While the money in question may, in fact, return by way of exports, there is no guarantee that this it will, especially if it is a member of another trade network. Second, despite being the instigator of the trading activity in question, whether directly or indirectly, the state will be unable to collect taxes from the third party.[16] If presented with the choice of two suppliers, one local, the other foreign, the government will choose the former, if only because it can tax its earnings, something it cannot do in the latter case. As the market (exclusive trading network) is, in essence, a government, it follows that foreign trade will be discouraged, as it undermines the government as the overseer of market activity by acting as a drain on its money (coinage) and on its tax revenues. Foreign merchants benefit from the market, created by government, but do not contribute to its creation via taxation. Put differently, they are free-riders.

Perhaps this explains the ubiquitous aversion to foreigners in ancient civilization. In other words, foreigners were the equivalent of non-members partaking in the activities of a club without paying the corresponding dues. Leo Oppenheim, in *Ancient Mesopotamia, Portrait of a Dead Civilization*, describes the role of foreigners as follows:

> It remains uncertain to what extent foreigners—non-citizens or non-natives—were admitted into the city. Typically, their status must have been diplomatic, that is, dependent on their relation to the palace. Foreign emissaries, traders, political refuges, and others were able to move in an out under royal protection or could even be incorporated into the royal household. It is probable that, to some extent, non-citizens were allowed to settle in the Karu, the harbor of the city, a section outside of the town proper. They enjoyed a special administrative, political, and social status. The institution of the "sojourners," or resident aliens, allowed to live within the city, which is known to us from the Old Testament, appears in Mesopotamia only in the west where a text from Ugarit speaks of "the citizens of the city of Carchemish together with the people (allowed to live) within their gates".... This contrasts with the Old Testament, where nomadic background can be readily adduced as explanations, but presents an instructive similarity to Greece—not the

Greece of Homer and its reflection in literature, but that of the polis, with its aversion to the non-citizen and all its discrimination, economic as well as social, against the alien. (Oppenheim 1964, 79)

Does this imply that foreign (extra-network) trade was altogether absent from the ancient economy? As it turns out, there are cases of foreign trade (i.e. across geo-political networks). What is important to point out, however, is that it was carried out by governments, and based on reciprocity.

3.6.3 Tariffs and Free-Riding

These findings suggest an alternative rationale for the existence of tariffs, namely as a means of internalizing an externality—in this case, the cost of making markets. In other words, tariffs, at least to begin with, would not have been developed as a means of discouraging trade, but rather as a means of collecting the government revenue that would otherwise have been lost (i.e. by dealing with foreigners)—in short, to internalize the externality that is benefiting from markets without having contributed. The tariff, in this case, represents the user's contribution to making markets.

An obvious consequence of such taxes is trade diversion, which is another way of saying, a reduction in foreign trade. The point, however, is that tariffs may not have been instituted so much as to reduce foreign trade, but instead, as a means of resolving the free-rider problem common to all public goods.

Such a view is implicit in Republican Senator Cullon's remarks in the U.S. Senate in the debate leading up to the Dingley Tariff Act:

> The initial policy and the groundwork of the enlightened universe is protection. The civilized world has grown out and away from barbaric free trade, and has developed a very universal recognition of the protective idea. In the savage state everything connected with human existence bears the impress of free trade and an unlimited and uncontrolled personal license. That condition allows the absolute equality and freedom of the individual, restrained alone by the physical strength and power of his fellow-savages.
>
> To him belongs everything, provided he can take and hold everything. His motto is "The world is mine," modified only by the limit of his physical ability. Out of the condition of savage freedom, and through the various stages of development and enlightenment time as brought into existence the family, the home, the society, the State, and the nation.
>
> And with this development and enlightenment the proper status of the individual became apparent. The preservation of his rights and the definition

of his duties demanded the establishment of the rules of society and the laws of civilized countries. The policy of union and cooperation in maintenance of law has become a fixed element in all modern governments. The people join together for mutual protection, and so joined together in societies, in municipal bodies, or in nations, they bear mutual burdens in order that they bear mutual benefits.

They waive a certain portion of their individual, natural rights, and the prerogatives which adhere to him in a savage state, that they may enjoy the mutual protection guaranteed by the government which they have established. They are joined in government establishment, as citizens of the same, and they owe their allegiance to that establishment in return for the protection it gives them. Violation of this allegiance is treason to the state. (*Senate Congressional Record*, April 27, 1894, 4166)

This provides an entirely different rationale for tariffs, namely as a means of internalizing the positive externality that is the creation—or making—of markets by governments. In other words, while citizens of the state pay for the making of markets via direct taxation (head tax, income tax), foreigners pay via indirect taxation (tariffs). A corollary comes in the form of the joint presence of multinational firms (transnational firms) and free trade. One could argue that the appearance of multinational firms rendered tariffs obsolete, in so far as the free-rider problem referred to here is concerned. By taxing the worldwide earnings of such firms, the free-rider problem disappears. Later, it will be argued that support of free trade in Great Britain and the United States was contemporaneous with the emergence of large British and American multinational firms, respectively.

3.6.4 Evidence: The Ancient and Modern Economies

These theoretical results, I maintain, are consistent with the historical record as presented in Chapter 2. The earliest evidence of large-scale specialization and exchange in the ancient economy coincides with the appearance of large-scale public goods, or what I refer to as "forced" trade. Moreover, civilizations, collective choice, public goods, cites, have, over the course of the last eight millennia, been synonymous. The introduction of fiat monies, and, more importantly, the requirement that taxes be paid in such monies, stimulated local trade. Citizens (members of the network) that did not trade directly with the government had to trade with those who did in order to secure the necessary coinage (fiat money). As governments—and cities—increased in size, so did their need for raw materials and energy (slaves). This led to the creation of trade networks, by persuasion or by force. As was shown in Chapter 2, most trade networks have been vertical in nature, involving the exchange of raw materials against finished goods. That network trade rarely involved the exchange of finished goods for finished goods owed to a number of factors, not the least of which was the technological advantage held by the center. Networks expanded in response to growing needs for raw materials, not for want of foreign finished goods. The historical record shows quite clearly that trade networks were forged by government, whether by plunder (force) or by negotiation.[17]

3.6.5 Trade and Geopolitical Borders

Further evidence of the important role geopolitical networks play in national and international trade, encouraging the former and discouraging the latter, comes from a recent findings on the role of borders (national, state, provincial, federal) on trade, and to a lesser degree migration. In 1995, John McCallum showed, much to everyone's surprise, that 1988 merchandize trade flows among Canadian provinces were twenty time as dense as those between Canadian provinces and U.S. states, after controlling for size and distance effects. This raised a number of questions, notably, if borders de facto matter—and matter a lot—for the world's two greatest trading partners, what about the rest of the world? Are border effects present elsewhere, and if so, of what magnitude? Shang-Jin Wei set out to answer this question, using 1982–1994 trade data for OECD countries. His results showed that an average country imports about two and a half times as much from itself as it does from an otherwise identical foreign country, again after controlling for a number of factors. In subsequent work, John Helliwell extended and reconciled McCallum and Wei's estimates, reporting border effects (last row) ranging from 8.6 to 21.1 are reported. As it turns out, these results are consistent with the model of geopolitical network trade presented here. In short, networks matter; moreover, networks matter a lot, for a number of reasons, not the least of which is the role/place of the network in the genesis of large-scale exchange. Geopolitical institutions have been and continue to play an important role in exchange.

Further contributing to strengthening "border effects" are the institutions of networks. Take, for example, financial institutions, which have, from the start, been the creations of the state (whether directly or indirectly—via the issuing of charters). The Bank of England is a case in point, being a government-sanctioned institution. The resulting geo-politically-based financial network, it follows, will have an important bearing on trade, favoring intra-geopolitical network trade, at the expense of "foreign trade."

These considerations, I argue, are what underlie the border effects reported by McCullum, Wei and Helliwell. As shown in Chapter 2, border effects have been synonymous with trade from the dawn of civilization. Well-defined geopolitical borders were, as shown earlier, a necessary condition for the rise of civilization and exchange.

3.7 The Institutions of Networks

In this section, I examine the institutions of networks. I argue that neural networks (networks based on information stored in the frontal cortex) assume a continuum of forms, from geopolitical integration (political and trade empires) to a business person's network of contacts (buyers and sellers). The former are examples of deep integration, while the latter are examples of shallow integration. Common to each is information on the buyer/seller, the good, the quality, the price, and other product (buyer/seller) attributes). Included on the continuum are such forms as geopolitical empires, trade associations, and multinational firms, the latter being a good example of a formal trade network that is economic, not geopolitical in nature.

The basic approach taken here is that of a correspondence. Specifically, it will be argued that neural networks map onto social networks. As such, social networks will mirror the exigencies of neural networks (neural trade networks). The choice among various types of social networks, it therefore follows, will depend on a number of factors, including the characteristics of the good/service being traded, and the characteristics of the agents themselves. For example, there is the nature of the trade, specifically, is the trade likely to be recurrent? If so, then one could argue that the agents will undoubtedly commit to a deeper form of social network, and vice versa. Another is whether the good/service in question is a public good. As shown in Chapter 2, the presence of a public good, with all that it entails, is more likely to result in deep forms of integration owing to the free-rider problem. There is no better illustration of this than the closing of geopolitical borders in the 1930's after the development of the welfare state. From that point on, immigration was closely monitored. Marriage with the purpose of procreation is another example, requiring, for the most part, a form of deep integration.

3.7.1 The Mechanics of Trade

As the basis of any and all neural networks, of which trade networks are an example, is information transmission, storage and retrieval, one could argue that, in the name of parsimony, members will develop common information transmission, storage and retrieval mnemonics, including language, culture, currencies, etcetera.

Language and Culture

As was argued in Chapter 2, early large-scale networks, including alliances among Cro-Magnon tribes and early Sumerian peoples, and symbolic mnemonics arose simultaneously. Put differently, culture, defined generally to include language, symbols, traditions, etcetera, is—and continues to be—a necessary condition for the emergence of networks. Without a system of writing and record keeping, civilization as we know it today (i.e. large-scale networks) would not have come about.

This leads me to argue that trading institutions, far from being after-thoughts, are an essential part of network formation, to the point of defining the network. These include a common language, a common legal framework, including common weights and measures, a common defense system, and a common currency. The historical record is replete with examples of shared trade-related institutions. The Roman empire (trade network) is a case in point. Member countries such as France, Belgium, and Spain all developed institutions that were Roman in their origins, including language, currency, judicial systems, and culture in general. The language spoken by the inhabitants of France today differs markedly from the language spoken two millennia ago, which was a combination of Celtic and German, the latter more present in the North. Latin was trade-enhancing (religion, government, commodities), and supplanted the local tongues. After centuries, the result was the French language which is spoken today, and, it bears noting, became itself, in the 16th and 17th centuries, a trade network language.

Language is, simply put, an exchange technology, mediating thoughts between individuals, actions not needing mediation, per se. It follows that different languages act as a barrier to trade. The case of the tourist in a foreign country with a different language illustrates the extent to which trade is hampered by different exchange technologies. It follows that to minimize transactions costs, a single language will be preferred to two or more. Remember that it (i.e. language) is a means, and not an end. What is being traded are thoughts, not words, the latter being the linguistic equivalent to money.

One could go as far as to argue that this simple fact underlies the history of language. Take, for example, the case of Quebec and the Mauritius islands, two former colonies. As pointed out earlier, trade networks are dynamic phenomena. Old trading networks are replaced by new ones, reflecting a new set of arbitrage opportunities. The cases of Quebec and Mauritius Islands, I believe, illustrate the role of language in network trade. To begin with, Quebec was a colony of France, providing valuable furs to the garments industry. French, as such, was spoken throughout what, at the time, was referred to as New France. French interest in the colony, however, waned, and in 1759, the British defeated a poorly-equipped French colonial army, to take the colony. Cast in terms of trade networks, this marked a realignment: Quebec would now be a part of the British trade network. Interestingly enough, however, English did not become the official language of Quebec. Business and trade would be conducted in English. Government and ecclesiastic affairs, however, would be conducted in French. This gave rise to a chasm between English Quebec which was, for the most part, involved in trade and commerce, that is, within the British trade network, and French Quebec, which was predominantly agrarian, Catholic and French speaking.

Quebec's language mosaic, one could argue, is the imprint—in the sense of mapping—of its colonial past, as is case of numerous colonies, including the Mauritius Islands, where English and French are also spoken, reflecting again, the influence of trade on institutions.

3.7.2 Network Membership, Learning and Opportunistic Behavior

The Roman empire can be regarded as an ideal, in so far as trade (money and markets) institutions are concerned. While the rest of the world was involved in subsistence farming, hunting and gathering, the Roman empire, like previous empires, had developed large-scale specialization, markets, and money.

People living on the frontier, I argue, would have been drawn to Roman life, with its high standard of living (provided one was not a slave). By choosing to become a part of the empire, a pagan sovereign would give up local autonomy in return for the right to adopt the institutions of the empire (money, markets, language, weights and measures, culture, etcetera).

This, of course, raises the question of opportunistic behavior. A sovereign could, strategically speaking, surrender control, and receive, in return, Roman civilization, and, then, sometime afterwards, revoke foreign control. Taxes would no longer be channeled to Rome (center), but would revert back to the newly created state (exclusive trade network). The point is that empires are, in essence, knowledge based, and, as such, are subject to the problems of knowledge in general, namely, opportunism. That is, individuals can join, acquire the information in question, and then defect, and establish a rival network.

3.8 Vertical Trade Networks

As shown in Chapter 2, large-scale trade networks have, from the very beginning, involved the exchange of raw materials for finished goods. Numerous are the cases in history in which trade has involved the exchange of value added (finished goods) for raw materials. The reasons for this are numerous, and include, among others, the appropriability of technology. While resources are, by definition, immobile, technology is not. This is as true of ancient Egypt as it is of 19th-century Great Britain.

The important point to note here is that within trade networks, the key determinants of trade were abundance (and quality) of raw materials, and technology, the former pertaining to the exporters of raw materials and the latter to the exporters of value added (finished goods). As both are non-stationary, it stands to reason that trade networks will also be non-stationary, changing with technology, resource endowments and time (population growth). In the next chapter, I develop a model of vertical trade (and, consequently, vertical trade networks) that is based on a simple model of production processes (value added). Namely, production consists of transforming (adding value to) raw materials or transformed raw materials. There are two universal inputs, namely broadly-defined energy and broadly-defined organization (Beaudreau 1998).

Broadly-defined energy consists of animate (muscular) energy forms as well as inanimate (fossil-fuel, solar, nuclear) ones. Broadly-defined organization consists of tools and supervision. For example, extracting raw materials requires energy and organization. In the ancient economy, animate, muscular (human) energy was used with primitive tools to extract various ores. In the 20th century, inanimate energy has replaced animate energy, resulting in multi-fold increases in output.

3.9 Conclusions

By way of a conclusion, I offer the following observations on the nature of our species, with particular reference to trade, defined generally to include socialization and trade in goods and services. The first is in response to the question raised in the previous chapter, namely "does the creation of a network precede or proceed trade?" or put differently, "are trade networks the formalization—institutionalization—of spontaneous trade, or are they a precondition for exchange?" As I have attempted to demonstrate in this chapter, causality runs, unequivocally, from public goods, to networks to large-scale specialization and exchange, owing in large measure to the nature of the underlying game, namely Nash. Spontaneous large-scale specialization and exchange could not have emerged in the absence of government, by which should be understood some form of communication and coordination device.

The nature of our species, specifically our propensity to "truck, barter and trade," owes, in large measure to our ability, developed over millions of years of evolution and speciation, to network and trade. The evidence, while still sparse, is unequivocal: large neo-cortexes are highly correlated with group size, the latter being a good proxy for socialization and trade. As Leonard Dudley has pointed out, "a community may be viewed as a group of individuals who acquire, store and exchange information."

The notion of free-trade (non-exclusive trade) is, as such, as an oxymoron. The notion that large-scale specialization and exchange can be spontaneous, in the sense of being devoid of government, is in direct violation of our nature, not to mention millions of years of evolution. We are, owing to our evolved brain, networkers by nature. To deny this is to ignore our fundamental nature. Free trade should, as such, be seen for what it was, namely political propaganda, aimed at dismantling one type of network, namely mercantile empires, and erecting, in its wake, a new type of empire, the economic—in this case, industrial—empire, based more so than ever before on the transformation of raw materials, but devoid of formal geopolitical ties.

As the historical record makes abundantly clear, network trade has, in most cases, been vertical in nature, involving the exchange of raw materials against finished goods. In the next chapter, a model of vertical trade is presented. In a world in which capital and labor are mobile, comparative advantage is shown to be determined by technology in the case of manufacturing, and the quality of the resources in the case of raw materials.

4

A Model of Vertical Trade

4.1 Introduction

The evidence presented in Chapters 2 and 3 is unequivocal: historically, large-scale trade has, for the most part, been organized in networks, and has invariably involved raw materials (i.e. intermediate inputs) and finished goods.[1] Cities have traded with contiguous and outlying regions. Industrialized regions have traded with resource-producing regions. Highly industrialized countries have traded and continue to trade with resource-rich countries. Clearly, the gains from vertical trade are ubiquitous. In this chapter, a model of vertical trade is presented. Given the nature of vertical trade (i.e. trade between the rows—as opposed to between the columns—of input-output matrices), it was felt that the underlying production processes was the best place to start (Hummels, Rapoport and Yi 1998; Hummels, Ishii and Yi 2001). Thus, in this chapter, I present a model of production activity which is vertical in nature, consisting of upstream resource producers and downstream transformers, both of which add value. By transformers, it should be understood all those who in some way or other add value to intermediate goods. Given the important role of growth in the history of trade and trading relationships, a dynamic version of the model is developed and used to study vertical trade over time (Findlay 1978). This allows for the study of phenomena such as site-switching, where downstream value-adders switch upstream raw material suppliers, thus prompting changes in any given vertical trade network (regional, national, and international).

4.2 The Prevalence of Vertical Gains from Trade

Judging from the archeological, evolutionary, and historical record, vertical gains from trade dwarf their horizontal equivalents as the leading cause of trade activity. Take, for example, the case of genetic evolution, specifically, the transition from RNA-based molecular growth to DNA-based molecular growth. According to Nobel Prize-winning biologist Christian deDuve:

> Scientists considering the origins of biological molecules confronted a profound difficulty. In the modern cell, each of these molecules (i.e., proteins and DNA/RNA) is dependent on the other two for either its manufacture or its function. DNA, for example, is merely a blueprint and cannot perform a single catalytic function, nor can it replicate on its own. Proteins, on the other hand, perform most of the catalytic functions, but cannot be manufactured without specifications encoded in DNA. One possible scenario for life's origins would have to include the possibility that two kinds of molecules evolved together, one informational and one catalytic. But this scenario is extremely complicated and highly unlikely.
> The other possibility is that one of these molecules could itself perform multiple functions. Theorists considering this possibility started to look seriously at RNA. For one thing, the molecule's ubiquity in modern cells suggests that it is a very ancient molecule. It also appears to be highly adaptable, participating in all the processes relating to information processing within the cell. For a while, the only thing that RNA did not seem capable of doing was catalyzing chemical reactions. That view changed when, in the late 1970's, Sydney Altman at Yale University and Thomas Cech at the University of Colorado independently discovered RNA molecules that, in fact, could catalytically excise portions of themselves or of other RNA molecules. The chicken-or-egg conundrum of the origin of life seemed to fall away. It now appeared theoretically possible that an RNA molecule could have existed that naturally contained the sequence information for its reproduction through reciprocal base pairing and could also catalyze the synthesis of more RNA strands. (de Duve 1995, 43)

Hence, as RNA evolved into DNA, it shed its catalytic role, which it would henceforth acquire via trade. From that point on, a catalyst and the DNA would combine to power molecular growth.

As pointed out in Chapter 2, the historical trade record is, in essence, about vertical trade. Throughout human history, raw materials have been traded against value added (transformation). Few finished goods were traded across borders. Only recently, with the rise of differentiated commodities (automobiles, clothes, electronic equipment) have horizontal trade and horizontal gains from trade become important.

4.3 A Descriptive Model of a Vertical Economy

Theoretically, a vertical economy can be reduced to two basic concepts, namely, raw materials and transformation, the latter being based—in keeping with the basic laws of the physical world—on energy, or, to be more precise, entropy. In this regard, industrial activity is no different from all other processes in the universe, including photosynthesis, cell growth, etcetera. In the case of photosynthesis, chlorophyll, by trapping the energy in sunlight, powers a series of chemical reactions, the end result of which is a sugar called glucose. In modern industry, energy, specifically electric power, is used to power a series of transformations (stages of value added), the result of which is the final good/service (Beaudreau .1998). Value is synonymous with transformation—untransformed feedstocks have little value, while transformed feedstocks have great value.

Equations 4.1–4.7 attempt to model the workings of an industrial economy—vertical trade network. I begin by assuming the existence of two geographical entities (e.g. cities, regions, countries), referred to as *manufacturia* and *primeria*. The first, defined by Equations 4.1 and 4.2, produces the finished product $y(t)$ using a Leontief-type technology (Equation 4.1) defined over $v(t)$, value added and $m(t)$, the intermediate input/product.[2] δ and γ are the relevant parameters. The greater is δ, the more more value added is required per unit output. Equation 4.2 describes *manufacturia*'s value-adding activities using the KLE value added production function developed in Beaudreau (1995).[3] Specifically, $ep(t)$ is electrical energy consumption (i.e. the energy input), $k(t)$ is the capital input and $l(t)$ is the labor input. Seen in this manner, *manufacturia* is engaged in the activity of adding value added ($v(t)$) to the intermediate input $m(t)$.

Equations 4.3 and 4.4 describe production of the intermediate product in the second geographical entity (e.g. *primeria*) in terms of a similar Leontief-type production function defined over $v_m(t)$, value added in the intermediate good sector, and $r(t)$, raw materials. As was the case in the first region, value added is modeled as an increasing function of $e_m(t)$, energy consumption in the second region, $k_m(t)$, the capital input in the second region, and $l_m(t)$, the labor input in the second region.

Note, however, that $\lambda(t)$, the input-output coefficient for $v_m(t)$, intermediate input value added, is a function of $R(0)$ and $R(t)$, the initial stock of the raw material, and the stock of the raw material at time t, respectively. This is based largely on the geological definition of a mineral deposit as the grade of the ore (i.e. $1/\lambda$) and the gross tonnage (i.e. $R(0)$). It will be argued that $\lambda(t)$, the relevant input-output coefficient, is decreasing in the former and increasing in the latter.

That is, the greater is the stock, *ceteris paribus*, the less value added (transformation) is needed to produce the intermediate input. On the other hand, the smaller is the stock (i.e. owing to site exhaustion), the more value added is needed to produce the intermediate input. For example, consider the case of iron ore. As higher grade ores are exhausted, the unit cost of producing a single ton of steel (pig iron) increases, as more electric power (energy) capital, and labor are required.

Equations 4.6 and 4.7 are the relevant Leontief price equations for the finished product and the intermediate product, respectively. The first defines P, the price of the finished product, as the sum of δP_v, the cost of value added per unit of output, and γP_m, the cost of the intermediate product per unit of output. P_v, the price of value added, is, in turn, determined by the price of factor inputs (e.g. energy, capital, and labor). P_m, the price of the intermediate good, is, as shown in Equation 4.7, a function of the price of value-added in the intermediate goods sector, as well as P_r, the price of the resource itself. The greater is λ, the greater is P_m, owing, as pointed out above, to site exhaustion.[4]

$$y(t) = min\left[\frac{v(t)}{\delta}, \frac{m(t)}{\gamma}\right]; \delta, \gamma > 0 \tag{4.1}$$

$$v(t) = A(t)ep(t)^{\alpha_1} k(t)^{\alpha_2} l(t)^{\alpha_3}; \alpha_1, \alpha_2, \alpha_3 > 0 \tag{4.2}$$

$$m(t) = min\left[\frac{v_m(t)}{\lambda[R(0),R(t)]}, \frac{r(t)}{\mu}\right]; \lambda[R(0),R(t)], \mu > 0 \tag{4.3}$$

$$R(t) = R(0) - \int_0^t r(\tau) d\tau \tag{4.4}$$

$$v_m(t) = A_m(t)ep_m(t)^{\beta_1} k_m(t)^{\beta_2} l_m(t)^{\beta_3}; \beta_1, \beta_2, \beta_3 > 0 \tag{4.5}$$

$$P = \delta P_v + \gamma P_m \tag{4.6}$$

$$P_m = \lambda[R(0),R(t)]P_{v_m} + \mu P_r \tag{4.7}$$

This descriptive model, I argue, captures the essential workings, both in time and in space, of an industrial economy, one based on entropy (transformation). The latter occurs in time, and in space, the former referring to the sequential nature of production activity, and the latter referring to its spatial nature. While *manufacturia* and *primaria* may be one in the same region, they have typically not been the same, owing to a number of factors, including site exhaustion, factor input localization, etcetera.

In a world of multiple *primarias* and *manufacturias*, it stands to reason that comparative advantage will be determined by cost conditions, and, as such, various price conditions, which, in turn, will be affected by the many parameters of the model. For example, the greater energy, capital, and labor productivity (total factor productivity) is, the lower the price of value added is, and, consequently, the lower the price of the intermediate and finished good is. As for *primarias* an important source of comparative advantage is site exhaustion. The more a site of a non-renewable raw material is worked over (exploited), the higher is the cost of producing a single unit of the intermediate product. A good example of this is the Mesabi iron range in Minnesota, which, owing to extensive mining operations in the first half of the 20th century, was no longer economically viable in the 1960's. All high-grade ores had been mined, leaving lower-quality, higher-cost taconite.

4.2.1 Dynamics

Equations 4.8–4.13 are the corresponding equations of motion of the model. Equations 4.8 and 4.10 describe the rate of growth of output in the two sectors as the lesser of the rate of growth of value added and the rate of growth of the intermediate input (the intermediate input in the case of the finished product and the raw material in the case of the intermediate input). Equations 4.9 and 4.11 describe the rate of growth of manufacturing value added and the intermediate input, respectively. Lastly, Equations 4.12 and 4.13 describe the relevant price dynamics.

$$\frac{\dot{y}(t)}{y(t)} = min\left[\frac{\dot{v}(t)}{v(t)}, \frac{\dot{m}(t)}{m(t)}\right] \tag{4.8}$$

$$\frac{\dot{v}(t)}{v(t)} = \alpha_1 \frac{\dot{ep}(t)}{ep(t)} + \alpha_2 \frac{\dot{k}(t)}{k(t)} + \alpha_3 \frac{\dot{l}(t)}{l(t)} \tag{4.9}$$

$$\frac{\dot{m}(t)}{m(t)} = min\left[\frac{\dot{v}_m(t)}{v_m(t)} - \frac{\dot{\lambda}(t)}{\lambda(t)}, \frac{\dot{r}(t)}{r(t)}\right] \tag{4.10}$$

$$\frac{\dot{v}_m(t)}{v(t)} = \alpha_1 \frac{\dot{ep}_m(t)}{ep_m(t)} + \alpha_2 \frac{\dot{k}_m(t)}{k_m(t)} + \alpha_3 \frac{\dot{l}_m(t)}{l_m(t)} \tag{4.11}$$

$$\dot{P} = \delta \dot{P}_v + P_v \dot{\delta} + \gamma \dot{P}_m + P_m \dot{\gamma} \tag{4.12}$$

$$\dot{P}_m = \lambda \dot{P}_{v_m} + P_{v_m} \dot{\lambda} + \mu \dot{P}_r + P_r \dot{\lambda} \tag{4.13}$$

These equations, especially Equations 4.8 and 4.10, serve to highlight the sectorial linkages that are characteristic of an industrial economy. Balanced growth requires that all sectors—in this case, *primaria* and *manufacturia*—grow at the same rate. Failure of one or the other to grow at comparable rates can be problematic, owing, in large measure, to Leontief aggregation.

As I shall go on to show in the next chapter, a large number of commercial conflicts had their roots in balanced growth, or, to be more precise, unbalanced growth. That is, the supply of intermediate inputs was oftentimes less than the supply of value added. The need to secure industrial feedstocks, history shows, has, oftentimes, led to conflict and war.

4.3 Sources of Industrial Growth

The model, as presented, is little more than a formalization of an input-output table. Linkages are identified and established. Questions relating to causality, are not included. In this section, I complete the model by examining the question of causality. The approach taken is taken from growth accounting, and consists, in general, of quantifying the contributions to growth of the various factor inputs, which, in my model, are energy, capital and labor. As economic growth is synonymous with the growth of a society's ability to transform raw materials, it follows that at issue are the causes of transformation growth.

The growth accounting literature is extensive, being based, in large measure on the pioneering contributions of Moses Abramovitz, Jan Tinbergen, and Edward Denison, to name but a few. The approach is relatively straightforward, namely starting with a standard Cobb-Douglas-like production function, deriving the equations of motion, and lastly, computing Divisia and/or Tornqvist indices using estimates of the various production parameters.

In most studies, the focus, as far as factor inputs are concerned, has been on capital and labor, and their variations. Exceptions include Ernst Berndt and David Wood's KLEMS model, where energy, materials and services are added to the list of factor inputs. In this section, I draw on earlier work of mine on the KLEP (capital, labor and electric power) production function.

4.3.1 The Rate of Growth of Post-WWII Manufacturing Value Added

In earlier work (Beaudreau 1995), I showed that by estimating the relevant fac-tor-input elasticities for the relevant KLEP (capital, labor and electric power) pro-duction function directly as opposed to indirectly (Gullickson and Harper 1988), (i) the Solow residual in U.S., Japanese and Canadian manufacturing in the post-WWII period disappeared; and (ii) that energy growth, measured by the rate of growth of electric power consumption, is the prime factor in output and produc-tivity growth. Table 4.1 presents the relevant least squares estimates of the KLEP production function output elasticities. We see that in all three cases, electric power is, by far, the prime factor input, followed by labor and capital. Electric power elasticities range from 0.533046 in U.S. manufacturing (1950–1984) to 0.728269 in Canadian manufacturing (1962–1988). Broadly-defined capital (i.e. plant and equipment) elasticities range from 0.033936 in Canada to 0.192974 in Japan.

Table 4.1
KLEP Regression Results U.S., Canadian and Japanese Manufacturing

Inputs	U.S. 1950–1984	Canada 1962-1988	Japan 1965–1988
EP	0.533046	0.728269	0.609444
	(10.079)	(4.493)	(3.067)
L	0.418822	0.249191	0.193766
	(18.231)	(2.332)	(1.847)
K	0.064250	0.0339365	0.193766
	(2.768)	(0.543)	(1.608)
R^2	0.984	0.968	0.981
F	1032.52	367.85	265.98

Source: Beaudreau (1995).

These estimates were then used to derive fixed-weight input growth indexes. These are shown in Table 4.2 where we see that in all three cases, three-factor input growth explains nearly all of the growth in manufacturing value added. The three-factor input growth index for U.S. manufacturing for the period 1950–1984 is 2.932 percent, while the actual growth rate is 2.995 percent. Similarly, the three-factor geometric index for Japan for the period 1965–1988 is 3.610, while the actual growth rate is 3.826 percent. Lastly, the three-factor geometric index for Canadian manufacturing for the period 1962–1988 is 3.037 percent, while the actual growth rate is 3.054 percent. What is noteworthy is the pronounced fall in the growth of electric power consumption in the post-OPEC period, and the resulting fall in the rates of growth of manufacturing value added in all three countries. Electric power consumption growth in U.S. manufacturing went from 6.226 percent prior to 1973 to 0.591 percent after. In Japanese manufacturing, it went from 11.320 percent to 0.965 percent, while in Canadian manufacturing, it went from 5.466 percent to 3.747 percent. As argued in my earlier work, the energy crisis, by decreasing the rates of growth of electric power consumption, constitutes the prime cause of the productivity slowdown.

Table 4.2
Input and Output Growth Rates, U.S., Japanese and Canadian Manufacturing

U.S.

	1950–1984	1950–1973	1974–1984
Value added(v)	2.995	4.217	0.330
Aggregate input	2.932	4.129	0.321
Electric power(ep)	4.455	6.226	0.591
Labor(l)	0.784	1.375	-0.503
Capital(k)	3.564	3.651	3.378

Japan

	1965–1988	1965–1973	1974–1988
Value added(v)	3.822	8.844	3.099
Aggregate input	3.610	8.494	2.916
Electric power(ep)	3.559	11.320	0.965
Labor(l)	-0.082	2.299	-0.367
Capital(k)	7.520	13.536	5.182

Canada

	1962–1988	1962–1973	1974–1988
Value added(v)	3.054	4.954	2.700
Aggregate input	3.037	4.575	2.843
Electric power(ep)	3.701	5.466	3.747
Labor(l)	0.834	1.703	0.344
Capital(k)	4.082	5.199	3.226

Source: Beaudreau (1995).

These results are convincing. Growth in energy consumption, measured here by electric power consumption, is a key determinant of economic growth, measured here by manufacturing value added. While at odds with the commonly held view that capital and labor are the key determinants of growth, these findings are, nonetheless, consistent with the basic laws governing physical processes, laws which underlie manufacturing process theory as seen by the engineering profession.[5]

4.3.2 The Rate of Growth of Post-WWII Intermediate Product Output

In this section, I examine the post-WWII developments in the production and consumption of two intermediate products, notably Copper and Primary Aluminum. Clearly, the post energy-crisis period (i.e. after 1973) was characterized by significantly lower rates of growth of intermediate good consumption.

Growth and Causality

Which of the two Leontief inputs in Equations 4.8 and 4.10 causes the rates of growth of final and intermediate products? Do increases in the rate of growth of intermediate products (raw materials) cause increases in the rate of growth of value added (intermediate product value added), and, eventually, the finished product (i.e. the manufacturing good and the intermediate product)? To answer this question, we turned to the business-cycle literature. Business cycle analysis identifies three types of indicators: leading, co-incident and lagging. It is a generally-accepted fact that in most market-oriented countries, manufacturing employment is a key leading indicator (Klein and Moore 1985).

Taken as a whole, the results of this extensive literature point to causality running from manufacturing employment to manufacturing value added to intermediate product value added to raw materials. In short, the key causal determinant of the rate of growth of raw materials is the rate of growth of manufacturing value added.

This is borne out by the various growth rates presented in Table 4.3, taken from Carmine Nappi's work on the aluminum and copper markets in the post World War II period. Table 4.3, which is constructed from data contained in Nappi (1990,1994), shows two distinct time sub-periods, notably 1960–1973 and 1973–1988(1991). In the former, OECD consumption of copper and primary aluminum increased at an average annual rate of 3.9 and 9.7 percent, respectively. From 1973–1988(1991), it increased at an average annual rate of 1.1 and 1.4 percent, respectively.

Table 4.3
Intermediate Product Growth Rates: Copper and Aluminum

Copper

	OECD	U.S.	Japan	ECC
1960–1973	3.9	3.3	10.2	2.3
1974–1988	1.1	1.2	2.3	0.4

Aluminium

	OECD	U.S.	Japan	ECC
1960–1973	9.7	9.6	20.0	10.0
1974–1988	1.4	-1.0	5.0	2.5

Source: Nappi (1990,1994).

We see that the rate of growth of intermediate good consumption tracks almost perfectly the rate of growth of manufacturing value added. For example, U.S. manufacturing value added increased from 1950–1973 at an average annual rate of 4.217 percent. Copper and primary aluminum consumption increased at average annual rates of 3.3 and 9.6 percent. From 1974–1984, the rate of growth of U.S. manufacturing value added decreased to 0.330 percent, resulting in a decrease in the rate of growth of copper to 1.2 percent and of primary aluminum to -1.0 percent.

In light of Equation 4.8, one can surmise that the resulting fall in the rate of growth of manufacturing value added (i.e. productivity slowdown) would have led to a decrease in the rate of growth of intermediate inputs, which in turn, would have led to a decrease in the rate of growth of intermediate product value added, and, of course, in the rate of growth of raw materials.

4.4 Industrial Growth and Trade

Thus far, I have ignored trade-related issues, focusing instead on the structure and dynamics of industrial output. The reason is simple: inter-regional and international vertical trade are, in the current era, as they were in antiquity, by-products of the process of industrial growth. Consider again the *manufacturia-primaria* dichotomization presented earlier. Equations 4.1, 4.2, 4.6, 4.8, 4.9 and 4.12 define and describe economic activity in *manufacturia*, while Equations 4.3, 4.4,

4.5, 4.7, 4.10, 4.11 and 4.13 define and describe economic activity in *primaria*. The latter is endowed with a raw material which requires energy, capital and labor to extract (and, perhaps, transform). The result (i.e. *m(t)*) is then traded to *manufacturia* where it is further transformed using electric power, capital and labor, the end product of which are manufactured commodities.

To model inter-regional and inter-national vertical trade, I begin by assuming the existence of *n* geographically-distinct *primaria*'s. That is, assume that the world consists of a single *manufacturia*, and *n primaria*'s. The latter may exist within a given geopolitical jurisdiction (i.e. country) or across geopolitical jurisdictions. In the former case, the resulting trade will be referred to as inter-regional trade, while in the latter it will be referred to as inter-national trade.

Suppose that the *n primaria*'s are arranged in increasing order of $\lambda(t)$. That is, *primaria(1)* has the lowest $\lambda(t)$, while *primaria(n)* has the highest $\lambda(t)$. For example, Russia's rich iron ore deposits place it among the first *primaria*'s, while France and Germany's would place it among the last *primaria*'s. Suppose that, to begin with, *manufacturia* trades with *primaria*. For example, in the 1930's and 1940's, the U.S. industrial heartland (i.e. the lower Great Lakes Region) traded with northern Minnesota (i.e. the Mesabi Iron Range). Growth in aggregate output is, as I have shown, determined, by the rate of growth of energy consumption in *manufacturia*. As *manufacturia* and *primaria* grow (i.e. at rate $v(t)/v(t)$), the initial stock of the non-renewable resource (i.e. *R(0)*) is used up, which, according to Equation 4.4, increases $\delta(t)$, the input-output coefficient. Each unit of the intermediate input requires progressively more value added. This pushes up the price of the intermediate product (see Equation 4.7), and ultimately, the final product (see Equation 4.6). Technically, this mimics what happens when the relevant resource deposit is exploited. As it is progressively exhausted (i.e. used up), more electric power, capital and labor are required to produce a single unit of the raw material (e.g. iron ore). As the cost of producing the intermediate product increases in *primaria*, there is reason to believe that given the presence of *n* − 1 other *primaria*'s, there will come a time (i.e. *t*) when *manufacturia* switches suppliers, opting for a lower-cost producer of intermediate product, in this case *primaria*. Marian Radetski, in *A Guide to Primary Commodities in the World Economy*, describes U.S. primary commodity imports in the past few decades as follows:

> In comparison with Japan and Western Europe, dependence on imported raw materials in the United States is still limited. The country's sparse population and vast resources made it into a large net exporter of commodities in aggre-

gate over long periods of time. In the past few decades, however, marginal deficits in U.S. non-fuel commodity trading have become more common. With increasing industrial needs and a gradual depletion of domestic resources, the net import needs are likely to increase over time. In the case of fuels, the deficit has already grown to a considerable value. (Radetski 1990, 19)

As the analysis shows, resource exhaustion (i.e. $\lambda(t)$ values) is not the only "switch" criterion. Other factors include the cost of processing raw materials in *primaria*. For example, while a country may be well-endowed in a particular raw material, it may lack the necessary infrastructure to make production economically feasible. This was the case in turn-of-the-century Quebec, where abundant forests and raw materials went unexploited for lack of infrastructure. As Claude Bellavance points out in his work on the development of the St-Maurice region of Quebec, it wasn't until foreign capital, primarily American, invested heavily in infrastructure, notably in hydroelectric development, that this region became a viable source of feedstocks (i.e. viable *primaria*). One could argue that recent investment activity on the part of U.S. mining multinationals in Russia is another case in point.

That this be the case should not come as a surprise. Inter-national trade has, since time immemorial, been the result of site-switching. Sumerian city-states, faced with growing raw material scarcity, turned to friendly—and not-so-friendly—city-states, in the hope of getting around such constraints. The Romans did likewise, turning to Northern Europe and Northern Africa for primary commodities.

4.5 Non-Vertical Trade

While vertical trade accounts for a large part of world trade, both past and present, it does not account for all of it. Countries also engage in what could be referred to as *manufacturia-manufacturia* trade, commonly known as intra-industry trade. That is, trade involving finished goods. For example, the United States exports automobiles to Sweden, and, in turn, imports automobiles from Sweden. This is sometimes referred to as trade in finished goods, or cross-hauling.

Such trade is determined by myriad factors, including tastes, technology, and relative prices. If we assume that *manufacturias* produce differentiated goods, and we assume that utility is increasing in product variety (i.e. Dixit-Stiglitz preferences), then trade can and will take place between manufacturias (Krugman 1980).[6]

Manufacturia-manufacturia trade, it therefore follows, can be understood in terms of differentiated products (resulting from research and development), economies of scale, and Dixit-Stiglitz preferences, in addition to price and cost considerations. referring to Equation 4.6, we see that the price of the finished product is the sum of the cost of manufacturing value added (i.e. δP_v), and the cost of the intermediate good (i.e. γP_m). The cost of manufacturing value added is, in turn, a function of the various factor productivities (i.e. the parameters of Equation 4.5) and the associated factor prices (electric power, capital and labor).

Comparative advantage, as far as differentiated products (horizontal trade) are concerned, will be determined by demand elasticities and cost considerations. *Manufacturia*s that have higher productivities/lower costs will advantaged, as will those that have access to cheaper intermediate goods (i.e. from the *primarias*).

Table 4.4
Determinants of Differentiated Product (Horizontal) Comparative Advantage

Product Related
Product-Based Research and Development
Advertising
Marketing
Cost Related
Process-Based Research and Development
Factor Costs
Intermediate Product Costs

4.5.1 Vertical Comparative Advantage

By industrial comparative advantage, it should be understood comparative advantage as determined by industry structure. *Primarias*, as such, will hold a comparative advantage in the up-stream processing of raw materials owing to (*i*) the very presence of the raw material, and (*ii*) the relative cost of extracting it. The latter is, in turn, a function of the quality of the raw material and, secondly, factor productivities and costs (i.e. the cost of transforming it). Conceivably, some regions or countries may possess higher quality resources, as measured by low values of λ, but be high cost producers owing to high-cost processing.

*Manufacturia*s will hold a comparative advantage in downstream processing activities, one based on a number of factors including what I choose to refer to as process and product technology. Included in process technology are down-stream production processes (physical processes) as well as down-stream distribution processes (e.g. marketing, networks, etcetera).[7] As broadly-defined energy and organization (capital and labor) are assumed to be mobile across regions and across countries, it stands to reason that region/country-specific comparative advantage will ultimately be based on (*i*) the quality of the resource endowment and (*ii*) the quality of process and product technology.[8]

Put more simply, resources and technology are the two key determinants of industrial comparative advantage. This, I believe, is borne out by the data, past and present. What made Great Britain the economic power its was in the 19th century was its technology, both process (production and distribution) and product. What makes Japan an economic power today is its technology, again both process and product. What made Canada rich in the 19th and 20th centuries was its natural resource base, what Canadian economic historian Harold Innis referred to as its "staples."

4.6 Vertical Trade Network Institutions

This section examines the institutional framework of vertical trade, the underlying idea being that such trade can be carried out in a number of various institutional arrangements, ranging from empires, to multinational firms, to arms-length transactions. Clearly, the choice of any particular institutional arrangement will depend, in large measure, on the exigencies of the particular case.

Table 4.5
Vertical Trade: Institutions

Geo-Political Empires
Spontaneous, Independent Markets
Integrated Multinational Firms

Perhaps the best way to study the choice of network institutions is to begin with the case of spontaneous trade in a world of *n primarias* and *n manufacturias*.[9] In such a case, markets (perfect) exist for the intermediate good ($m(t)$), the final good ($y(t)$), value added in both sectors ($v(t)$, $v_m(t)$), and for the factor inputs. With a sufficiently large n, it stands to reason that inter-regional (or international trade) trade would be spontaneous in nature, and, moreover, be competitive in nature.

Such a view, however, stands in stark contrast with the historical record, where vertical trade has, for the most part, been conducted within well-defined networks. This raises a number of questions, not the least of which is why? Why has vertical trade, from the dawn of civilization (Ancient Mesopotamia), been carried out in what are "deep" networks, namely geopolitical networks and multi-national firms? Rare are the instances in which vertical trade was carried out out-side of the relevant geopolitical network. Witness the dearth of spot markets for raw materials.

Putting aside, for the moment, the case of geopolitical empires, the question can be framed as follows, namely, why is it that manufacturing firms in the 20th century were, for the most part, large vertically-integrated, oftentimes multina-tional, entities, with upstream and downstream holding? The automobile indus-try is a good example. Why did what Alfred Chandler refers to as the "Visible Hand" of management usurp Adam Smith's "Invisible Hand?"

In the answer to this question lies the answer to the question at hand, namely, what determines the choice of vertical trade institution? Clearly, the forces which gave rise to highly-integrated manufacturing (upstream and downstream) would be the same that gave rise to the multinational firm, which is nothing more than the former set in a multi-national setting. That is, an integrated firm that knows no geopolitical boundaries. Put differently, why have firms chosen opted to "internalize" vertical trade? As it turns out, there is an abundant literature on the subject (Chandler 1977; Caves 1982; Dunning 1981). Included among the causes are such things as transactions costs, market imperfections, asymmetric information, etcetera.[10] I, however, would like to focus on what I believe are, his-torically speaking, some determining factors. First, there is what I refer to as the knowledge asymmetry, defined in terms of process and product technology. In most cases in recorded history, to begin with, *primaria* and *manufacturia* were one in the same. The Sumerian city-state is a case in point. To begin with, raw materials and value added were present within the same geopolitical confine. Population growth combined in the presence of resource exhaustion forced the priests/governors of city-states to look abroad for new supplies of raw materials. The problem, however, was that, in most cases, neighboring geopolitical entities (e.g. city-states, countries, regions, tribes) had reached the same level of develop-ment, making for a situation in which nowhere was the raw material in question being worked (i.e. processed).

This left a number of options, including negotiating with the peoples on whose territory the raw materials in question were located on the one hand, and political annexation via military invasion on the other. As it turns out, the latter strategy appears to have been the preferred one, as history bears witness.

The knowledge asymmetry can also be invoked to explain the presence of upstream vertically-integrated multinationals in third-world countries. Again, natural resource bottlenecks at home (e.g. U.S., Germany, France, Great Britain) have forced producers—and countries—to seek out new supplies, whether by way of arms-length transactions or by direct investment/involvement. Again, as history bears witness, the preferred—and, indeed, only—route was direct investment/involvement, owing to the knowledge asymmetry. A case in point is the case of the Iron Ore Company of Canada, a U.S.-based multinational created in the mid-1950's with the express purpose of tapping northern Quebec's rich veins of iron ore. Here, the absence of Canadian-owned and -operated mining companies lies at the root of the decision on the part of U.S. steel producers to develop the raw material in question themselves. What is interesting to note is that nearly 100 percent of the iron ore produced in Quebec is exported to the United States.

It can also be invoked to explain—rationalize—the presence of downstream vertically-integrated multinationals in developed countries. In this case, the knowledge asymmetry in question is related to the distribution (marketing) of what, in most cases, is a new product. A new product is developed say in the United States, for which an important market exists in Europe. Unfortunately, however, no one in Europe is sufficiently qualified to market (distribute) the product, with the result that the U.S. producer has to open a sales office in the host country. A good example of this is the U.S. electric power equipment industry's (General Electric and Westinghouse) early experience in Europe, where, owing to the novelty of the product, they were forced to open up sales offices, complete with technical staff.

Another factor contributing to the emergence of trade networks is security of supply. As the model presented above makes clear, raw materials and value added are complementary inputs, making for a situation in which absence of one necessarily implies absence of the other. In a perfectly competitive raw materials marketplace, with many sellers and buyers, security issues would be non-existent. The reality, however, is that these markets are rarely competitive (Radetzki 1990). In most cases, spot markets do not exist. This makes for a case in which security issues are highly relevant. According to Marian Radetzki (1990), "When the importer is heavily dependent on foreign sources, and when the commodity if not easily substituted in critically important uses, severe damage may be caused by a disturbance in international supply (Radetzki 1990, *xi*). Downstream producers will, as such, want to ensure a continuous, reliable supply of feedstocks, and, consequently, will choose to either enter long-term contracts with suppliers, or direct invest.

A good example of the risks associated with arms-length transactions is the U.K. textile industry in the post-Civil War period. From 1800 to 1860, U.S. cotton exports to the textile manufacturers of the northern England towns of Manchester, Leeds, Liverpool, etcetera increased dramatically. This symbiotic relationship, however, came to an abrupt end after the Civil War, when exports to the U.K. were cut off, contributing to a severe downturn in the U.K. Clearly, in this case, the market had failed Britain, for textile producers were unable to, on short notice, replace U.S. cotton.

4.6.1 The Government's Problem

It goes without saying that governments (i.e. elected officials) in both regions (*manufacturia* and *primaria*) have a vested interest in fostering good trade relations. A breakdown of trade between the regions would be catastrophic for obvious reasons. One need only consider Japan's plight were it to be cut off from its sources of energy and raw materials. In this section, I examine the question of optimal trade policy in light of (*i*) the model of vertical trade presented above, and (*ii*) fiscal concerns (i.e. those raised in Chapter 2).

It is clear that the government's interests are twofold, namely (*i*) ensuring the smooth and continuous operation of the region's productive factors (wealth), and (*ii*) collecting tax revenues for what I refer to as "making the market." As pointed out in Chapter 2, the latter is synonymous with public goods.

Let me begin with the latter concern. First, consider the case of the Roman empire, where the provision of public goods lay at the origin of market activity. Without public goods, markets would not exist. The cost of such markets, it therefore follows, was the taxes its citizens paid. Faced with resource bottlenecks, Rome could have instituted free trade with, say, Northern Africa, or with Gaul. The problem, however, is that in doing so, it would be creating a class of citizens that, in keeping with the public finance literature, can best be described as "free-riders," in the sense that they would benefit from Roman markets without paying their "fair share." To overcome this problem, it could theoretically impose an import tax, the incidence of which would fall either on the importer or exporter.

Or, it could simply internalize the free-rider problem by annexing the country. In this case, the conquered country is formally annexed (geo-politically) and, as such, pays taxes to Rome—put differently, pays its "fair share." Historically, this appears to have been the preferred solution.

4.6.2 Inter-Network Trade and Multinational Firms

Historically, inter-network trade has been discouraged. For example, leaders of Greek city-states discouraged trade with neighboring city-states. More recently, the British empire discouraged trade with the French and Spanish empires. Today, the European community discourages trade with the United States and Japan, encouraging trade, however, between member countries.

As I have shown, extra-network trade weakens the network by acting as a leak-age on network income. While imports from other networks may, in fact, be matched by exports, there always exists the very real possibility that they will not, in which case the overall level of income (trade) in the network in decreased.

The multinational firm has emerged as the dominant vertical trade network institution in the 20th century, marking a paradigm change from the past where geopolitical empires were, for the most part, the norm. The result is a world in which vertical trade networks are no longer geopolitical in nature, but, instead, are economic. Governments have, over the course of the 20th century, reduced import taxes (tariffs), with the result that today tariff revenues in most countries have decreased considerably. Multiple empires (i.e. multinational firms) can now coexist in the same geopolitical entity, resulting in the present situation which I refer to as that of overlapping trade networks. Multinational firms crisscross one another in any given geopolitical entity. Take, for example, the case of Canada, where Japanese, American, and European multinationals coexist, providing a striking contrast with Canada at the time of either the British or French colonial empires.

What happened to the "free-rider" problem referred to above? Has free-trade not re-introduced as it were the problem? Are not foreigners who export not free-riding on the "public good" which is the market? The answer is no, at least in so far as the vertically-integrated multinational firm is concerned. The reason owes to the fact that the home (source) country taxes worldwide profits, not just profits earned in the country in question. In a world dominated by multinationals that pay income taxes on worldwide income (profits), the free-rider problem disappears. This may explain why governments the world over actively promote domestic multinationals. The better country A's multinationals do abroad, the greater the tax revenues, and the greater the social good (public goods).

Network Hierarchies

Not all networks are equal. Some may dispose of more abundant resources and more efficient transformation processes, leading to absolute and perhaps even comparative advantage. For example, the United Kingdom in the 19th century dominated the world trade network hierarchy with its abundant raw materials and efficient (due to the steam engine) transformation processes.

Inter-Network Trade and Multinational Firms

The existence of relative price differences across countries and networks will, in the presence of trade barriers or not, lead to inter-network exchange. The latter can assume two forms, namely trade where goods and services are exchanged, or foreign direct investment (multinational firms) where manufacturers from one trade network invest in another. A good example of this is U.S. foreign direct investment in Great Britain—and Europe in general—in the 1920's and 1930's.

Clearly, the presence of inter-trade network foreign direct investment will be perceived of as a threat to the long-term survival of the host trade network. Such threats are typically framed in terms of national sovereignty. Multinational firms are less likely to encourage intra-host trade network exchange, which would contribute to weakening the network. Their presence in the host country may—but need not—jeopardize local manufacturers, the backbone of the vertical trade network.

One could argue that economic nationalism is, in essence, a defensive response to inter-trade network exchange. For example, the presence of Japanese multinationals in Europe has irritated and continues to irritate European nationalists.

4.7 Summary

Unlike existing models of international trade that view trade as involving finished goods only, this chapter presented a model of trade based on a dynamic model of output growth, providing a framework to understand at least eight thousand years of world trade. The resulting trade, in keeping with the historical record, is industrial in nature, involving raw materials and energy for value added (transformation).

Mediating trade activity are the terms of trade; that is, the terms of trade between *manufacturia* and *primaria*. As shall soon become apparent (in the next chapters), vertical trade networks are highly sensitive to variations in the terms of trade. In recorded history, variations in the terms of trade have prompted many important geopolitical changes.

5

International Trade: The Evidence

We must find new lands from which we can easily obtain raw materials and at the same time exploit the cheap slave labor that is available from the natives of the colonies. The colonies would also provide a dumping ground for the surplus goods produced in our factories.

—Cecil Rhodes, 1853–1902

5.1 Introduction

What is particularly interesting about this quote, attributed to Cecil Rhodes, is the implied duality. On the one hand, he refers to Great Britain's need for raw materials, which is consistent with the vertical model of trade presented above. On the other hand, the trade he refers to occurs within the context of a geopolitical economic network, namely the British Commonwealth. In this chapter, the model of trade presented in the previous chapter is tested against the data. Is there evidence that trade is both vertical and horizontal as pointed out in the previous chapter? Do the exigencies of highly complex industrial processes determine trade relations? To what extent is trade horizontal in nature? Does trade take place in well-defined networks? Do geopolitical borders (geopolitical networks) affect trade?

To answer these and other questions, I proceed as follows. To begin with, I examine the question of vertical and horizontal international trade. What are the underlying determinants of vertical and horizontal trade? What are the implications for the factor content of trade? Do the data corroborate the predictions of the model? This is then followed by various tests of the role of networks in trade. Among these are the results of the "border effects" literature that dates back to John McCallum's seminal 1995 *American Economic Review* paper.

5.2 Vertical and Horizontal Trade: The Evidence

5.2.1 Comparative Advantage

As pointed out in Chapter 4, by comparative advantage, it should be understood the comparative advantage of a region or country as determined by its endowments. *Primarias* will have a comparative advantage in the up-stream processing of raw materials owing to (1) the presence of the raw material, and (2) the relative cost of extracting it. The latter is, in turn, a function of the quality of the raw material—typically measured in terms of resource concentrations (ores, fibers, etcetera)—and, secondly, the processing cost (i.e. extracting it). Conceivably, some regions or countries may have higher quality resources, as measured by low values of λ, but be high cost producers owing to relatively higher processing costs. *Manufacturias* will have a comparative advantage in downstream processing activities, one that is based on a number of factors pertaining to process and product technology. Included in process technology are production processes per se (engineering) as well as distribution processes (e.g. marketing, networks, etcetera).[1]

As broadly-defined energy and organization are assumed to be mobile across regions and across countries, it stands to reason that region/country-specific comparative advantage will be based on country-specific factors such as the quality of the resource endowment and the quality of process and product technology.[2] Put more simply, resources and technology are the two key determinants of comparative advantage. As such, comparative advantage is both exogenous and endogenous, the former corresponding to resource endowments, and the latter corresponding to broadly-defined technology.

Table 5.1
Manufacturia **Correlates**

Product Research and Development
Advertising
Marketing Distribution Networks Headquarter Activity Finance
Predominantly Urban

5.3 Industrial Structure Correlates

Leaving aside, for the moment, the question of causality, I examine, in this section, the question of industrial structure correlates—that is, the structural characteristics of regions and countries (i.e. *manufacturias* and *primarias*). For example, *manufacturias* are, relative to *primarias*, more likely to engage in research and development and advertising activity. *Primarias*, on the other hand, are less likely to engage in these activities owing, in large measure, to the nature of their product, namely being homogeneous in nature.

Table 5.2
Primaria **Correlates**

Raw Materials
Abundant Energy
Bulk Transport Systems
Predominantly Rural (Low Population Density)

Given the presence of non-negligible transportation costs and resource concentration levels that are oftentimes less than 100 percent, it stands to reason that, unlike processing activities in *manufacturias*, processing activities in *primarias* are not footloose. That is, they have to be carried out in the region. Subsequent transformation can, however, be carried out elsewhere. Examples of this are mining, forestry, and agricultural activities. Processing activity in *manufacturia* is, in general, footloose, although, historically, there have been numerous exceptions. Take, for example, the case of manufacturing in the United States in the 19th century, which, owing to the power drive technology—hydraulics—was localized chiefly in New England (the eastern Appalachian watershed). One could go as far as to argue that transformation-based activities, like resource-based activities, are specific to regions, owing in large measure to the cultural (read: public good) nature of activities such as research and development. If innovation is partly cultural, then it stands to reason that production processes that are innovation intensive will be region-specific (Beaudreau 1989). Silicon valley in California is a case in point.

5.3.1 Non-Traditional Factor Intensities by Industry

By non-traditional factor intensities, it should be understood factor intensities other than those typically reported in the literature (capital, labor, energy, land, etcetera). For a listing of these, see Bowen, Leamer, and Sveikauskas (1987), and Trefler (1995). Among the non-traditional factor intensities are what some writers have referred to as the innovation intensity or innovation quotient. Some industries are more innovation intensive than others. The electronics industry is a case in point. Expenditure on research and development measured as a percentage of total sales in electronics is as high as six percent, which dwarfs expenditure in, say, primary metals.

It therefore stands to reason that for a firm, region, or country to compete in the electronics industry, a company/region/country must be well-endowed in innovation, and its tributary activities (universities, technical institutes, etcetera). Table 5.3, presented below, presents research and development intensities by two-digit industry. We see, for example, that up-stream, raw material-related industries (i.e. *primaria*) such as Petroleum and Coal Products, Lumber, Wood Products, and Primary Metal Industries are less research and development intensive than down-stream manufacturing industries such as Transportation Equipment, Instruments and Related Products, and Electronic Equipment.

5.3.2 Traditional Factor Intensities by Industry

In this section, I examine the traditional factor content of trade, focusing particular attention on three factor intensities, namely the electric power (energy), capital and labor intensities in the intermediate input-producing sector and the manufacturing value-adding sector. The data show the former, taken as a whole, to be electric power (energy) and capital intensive relative to the former, and the latter to be labor intensive. This implies that exports from *primarias* will, in general, be electric power (energy) and capital intensive, while exports from *manufacturias* will be labor intensive. A case in point is aluminum refining which is highly energy and capital intensive. Refined ingots of aluminum will, as such, be highly energy and capital intensive.

Factor Intensities by Industry

The model of final-product value added and intermediate product-value added focuses on three factor inputs: research and development, electric power, capital and labor (i.e. the KLEP production function; see Beaudreau (1995)). In this section, I report factor intensities for 14 2-digit SIC industries. Table 5.3 presents three factor intensities for each of the 14 2-digit SIC industries, specifically the ratio of research and development expenditure to overall sales, electric power consumption to labor and the ratio of capital to labor. The results show clearly that intermediate products are, on the whole, more electric power and capital intensive and less research and development intensive than final products. For example, the capital-labor and electric power-labor ratios in SIC 29, Petroleum and Coal Products, SIC 26, Paper and Allied Products, and SIC 33, Primary Metal Industries, two low R&D industries, are $169,808 and 377,521 kwh per worker, $58,443 and 154,278 kwh per worker, and $58,407.28 and 205,442 kwh per worker, respectively. Conversely, in SIC 36, Electric and Electronic Equipment, SIC 37 Transportation Equipment, and SIC 35, Machinery, except Electrical, two high R&D industries, these ratios are $14,473 and 20,870 kwh per worker, $20,775 and 24,717 kwh per worker, and $18,500 and 19,248 kwh per worker, respectively.

5.4 Industrial Interregional and International Trade

As pointed out earlier, nations and countries, especially federations and confederations, often consist of a number of distinct regions, some of which process raw materials (i.e. *primarias*), while others process intermediate goods (i.e. *manufacturias*). Trade among these regions, I maintain, is vertical in nature.[3] In this section, the interregional industrial trade of the United States is examined. However, as regional trade data are not available, the relevant unit of analysis is the state. States will, as such, be classified as being either predominantly a *primaria* or a *manufacturia*.[4]

Table 5.3
Two-digit SIC Industry Factor Intensities

SIC	Industry	R&D	k/l ($)	e/l (kwh)
20	Food and Kindred Products	0.4	40,801	39,756
22	Textiles and Apparel	0.4	9,453	21,149
24	Lumber, Wood Products	0.8	12,657	28,339
26	Paper and Allied Products	0.9	58,443	154,278
28	Chemicals and Allied Products	3.6	107,263	266,175
29	Petroleum and Coal Products	0.7	169,808	377,521
30	Rubber and Misc. Plastic Products	2.4	24,403	39,788
32	Stone, Clay and Glass Products	1.2	35,431	64,297
33	Primary Metal Industries	0.8	58,407	205,442
34	Fabricated Metal Products	1.2	16,969	20,686
35	Machinery	5.0	18,500	19,248
36	Electronic Equipment	6.3	14,473	20,870
37	Transportation Equipment	3.1	20,775	24,717
38	Instruments and Related Products	5.6	16,704	16,149

Source: Beaudreau (1989).

5.4.1 Industry Correlates by State

Whether a state will produce and export intermediate goods (*primaria*) or finished goods (*manufacturia*) will depend on a number of factors, not the least of which are its resource endowment, and its level of research and development. States with important resource endowments will, in general, produce and export intermediate goods (i.e. transformed raw materials). On the other hand, states with high levels of research and development, it stands to reason, will produce and export finished goods. States with both will produce and export both.

Table 5.4
Total R&D and GSP, by State: 1997

Rank	State	Total R&D	GSP	Percent	Rank	Percent
	U.S.	211,268				
1	California	41,670	1,033,016	4.03	9	19.72
2	Michigan	13,991	272,607	5.13	3	6.62
3	New York	12,307	651,652	1.89	25	5.83
4	New Jersey	12,067	294,055	4.1	8	5.71
5	Massachusetts	11,097	221,009	5.02	4	5.25
6	Texas	9,487	601,643	1.58	28	4.49
7	Pennsylvania	8,209	339,940	2.45	15	3.89
8	Illinois	8,034	393,532	2.04	21	3.8
9	Washington	7,543	172,253	4.38	6	3.57
10	Maryland	7,395	153,797	4.81	5	3.5
11	Ohio	7,145	320,506	2.23	17	3.38
12	Florida	4,784	380,607	1.26	31	2.26
13	North Carolina	4,667	218,888	2.13	18	2.21
14	Virginia	4,136	211,333	1.96	23	1.96
15	Minnesota	3,605	149,394	2.41	16	1.71
16	Connecticut	3,454	134,565	2.57	12	1.63
17	Colorado	3,205	126,084	2.54	13	1.52
18	Indiana	3,149	161,701	1.95	24	1.49
19	New Mexico	3,028	45,242	6.69	1	1.43
20	DC	2,768	52,372	5.29	2	1.31
21	Arizona	2,410	121,239	1.99	22	1.14
22	Georgia	2,272	229,473	0.99	38	1.08
23	Wisconsin	2,256	147,325	1.53	30	1.07
24	Missouri	1,826	152,100	1.2	33	0.86
25	Alabama	1,637	103,109	1.59	27	0.77
26	Tennessee	1,566	146,999	1.07	36	0.74
27	Oregon	1,520	98,367	1.54	29	0.72
28	Utah	1,381	55,417	2.49	14	0.65
29	Kansas	1,351	71,737	1.88	26	0.64
30	Idaho	1,270	29,149	4.36	7	0.6

31	Delaware	1,089	31,585	3.45	11	0.52
32	Rhode Island	1,040	27,806	3.74	10	0.49
33	South Carolina	1,040	93,259	1.11	35	0.49
34	Iowa	980	80,479	1.22	32	0.46
35	New Hampshire	799	38,106	2.1	19	0.38
36	Oklahoma	644	76,642	0.84	40	0.3
37	Louisiana	554	124,350	0.45	50	0.26
38	Kentucky	526	100,076	0.53	46	0.25
39	Nevada	517	57,407	0.9	39	0.24
40	West Virginia	427	38,228	1.12	34	0.20
41	Mississippi	370	58,314	0.63	43	0.17
42	Vermont	314	15,214	2.06	20	0.15
43	Nebraska	275	48,812	0.56	44	0.13
44	Hawaii	275	38,024	0.72	42	0.13
45	Arkansas	272	58,479	0.46	49	0.13
46	Montana	199	19,160	1.04	37	0.09
47	Maine	149	30,156	0.49	48	0.07
48	Alaska	136	24,494	0.55	45	0.06
49	North Dakota	116	15,786	0.73	41	0.05
50	Wyoming	87	17,561	0.5	47	0.04
51	South Dakota	71	20,186	0.35	51	0.03

Table 5.4 presents various R & D—related statistics by state for 1997. We see, for example, that California, Michigan, New York, New Jersey and Massachusetts account for 43 percent of total research and development expenditure in the United States, which, in 1997, stood at $211.268 billion. At the bottom of the list are South Dakota, Wyoming, Alaska, and Maine.

As can be seen, California, Michigan, New York, New Jersey, Massachusetts, Texas, Pennsylvania, Illinois and Pennsylvania rank among the leading *manufacturia* states in the United States, accounting for, 60 percent of total research and development expenditure in the United States. Conversely, South Dakota, Wyoming, North Dakota, Alaska, Maine, Montana, Arkansas and Hawaii rank among the leading *primaria* states, being, for the most part, dependent on their resource base for generating wealth, in this case, intermediate goods.

Our model would predict that trade between states such as California, Michigan, and Massachusetts, on the one hand, and South Dakota, Wyoming, and North Dakota on the other hand would be vertical in nature, while trade between California, Michigan, and Massachusetts would be horizontal in nature. Put differently, trade between these states would be intra-industry in nature (cross-hauling).

5.5 The Factor Content of International Trade

In this section, I examine the factor content of vertical and horizontal international trade. How do upstream and downstream transformers/countries differ in so far as relative factor intensities are concerned. Are resource-exporting countries more labor, capital, and/or energy intensive, relative to manufacturing goods-exporting countries? Are resource-exporting countries less research and development intensive, relative to manufacturing goods-exporting countries? I begin with the case of five countries, notably Canada, U.S., Japan, Australia and Norway.

The measures of the electric power, capital and labor factor intensities of final and intermediate products (Table 5.3) were used in combination with trade data for 110 countries to generate descriptive summary measures of the factor content of trade between *manufacturia*'s and *primaria*'s.

Table 5.5
Factor Content of Trade: U.S., Japan, Canada, Australia, and Norway

Ratio	U.S.	Japan	Canada	Australia	Norway
R&D$_{exports}$	2.79	3.51	1.95	0.93	1.44
R&D$_{imports}$	2.04	1.14	2.93	2.94	2.54
k/l$_{exports}$	40,278	25,086	60,047	60,378	105,228
k/l$_{imports}$	81,065	116,396	41,210	53,436	56,016
e/l$_{exports}$ (*kwh*)	75,335	43,083	126,795	113,909	236,849
e/l$_{imports}$(*kwh*)	173,257	254,383	80,355	108,287	114,719

These consist of simple weighted averages, with the weights being the sector's share of exports/imports in total country exports/imports. Table 5.5 presents the results for five of these countries, namely Canada, the United States, Japan, Australia, and Norway. The U.S. and Japan were chosen as examples of the former, while Canada and Australia and Norway were chosen as examples of the latter.[5] We see that the U.S. and Japan's exports are, relatively speaking, more R&D intensive than those of the three other countries. We also see that the U.S. and Japan's exports are substantially less capital and electric power intensive than those of the three *primaria*'s, while their imports are more capital and electric power intensive than those of these same three countries. U.S. exports are more capital and electric power-intensive than U.S. imports. The capital-labor and electric power-labor ratios for U.S. exports are $40,278 and 75,33kwh, respectively, which literally dwarfs the corresponding U.S. import ratios of $75,335 and 173,257kwh, respectively. Compare this with either Canada, Australia or Norway, where the reverse holds. These cursory measures confirm Leontief (1953) and Vanek (1963)'s findings regarding the factor content of U.S. foreign trade. Specifically, U.S. exports are more labor intensive than U.S. imports; U.S. imports are more capital intensive than U.S. exports.

Interestingly, Japan's exports are more R&D intensive and more labor intensive than the U.S.'s. This, one could argue, results from the very nature of Japan's international trade, namely as being predominantly vertical in nature. That is, Japan's intra-industry trade is, comparatively speaking, less than the U.S.'s. Japan's imports are predominantly vertical in nature.

5.5.1 The Factor Intensity of Trade: The General Case

Similar results were obtained for the 105 other countries listed in Table 5.6, where three factor intensity measures are presented. The first is the ratio of the R&D content of exports to the R&D content of imports, while the second is the ratio of the capital/labor ratio of exports to the capital/labor ratio of imports. The third is the ratio of the electric power/labor ratio of exports to the electric power/labor ratio of imports. Values greater than one indicate that the country in question is a net exporter of either R&D, capital or electric power. Values less than one of R&D indicate that the country is a net importer of research and development. Likewise, values of the capital/labor and electric power/labor ratio less than one indicate that the country is a net importer of capital and electric power, respectively, and a net exporter of labor. Once again, the countries divide along factor intensity lines, with *manufacturias* being net exporters of research and development and labor, while *primarias* being net exporters of capital and energy in the form of electric power. The Group of Six (G-6) countries are net exporters of research and development, and net importers of capital and electric power. This is not surprising; in fact, it is predicted by the theory. Highly industrialized economies are net exporters of their know-how and labor, while resource-based economies are net exporters of capital and electric power (energy).

Table 5.6
Factor Content of Trade

Country	$R\&D_{1978}$	K/L_{1978}	E/L_{1978}
Afghanistan	0.139296	1.734469	1.553326
Algeria	1.197633	0.701748	0.694112
Argentina	0.254041	0.925864	0.685999
Australia	0.316109	1.204025	1.309904
Austria	1.059126	0.597491	0.644605
Bangladesh	0.225636	0.290352	0.228108
Belgium-Luxembourg	1.087999	0.806263	0.836120
Belize	0.237553	0.545203	0.294494
Benin	0.227708	0.962845	0.542161
Bolivia	0.204072	1.723181	2.327743
Brazil	0.859222	0.414197	0.357569
British Virgin Islands	0.705558	0.488519	0.416753
Bulgaria	0.705711	0.706609	0.521595
Burma	0.195572	0.886165	0.554160
Burundi	0.213169	0.568461	0.278484
Canada	0.769832	1.084426	1.149509
Central African Republic	0.311729	0.739121	0.594202
Chad	0.286149	0.482828	0.433554
Chile	0.367582	0.845901	1.255674
Colombia	0.276779	0.734514	0.441065
Cook Islands	0.229505	0.799291	0.421048
Costa Rica	0.476247	0.753534	0.492964
Cuba	0.222552	0.470132	0.246174
Cyprus	0.599331	0.641494	0.531398
Czechoslovakia	1.353644	0.530379	0.496223
Denmark	1.059866	0.470512	0.368508
Dominica	0.467396	0.971854	0.736985
Dominical Republic	0.319279	0.521154	0.379522
Ecuador	0.181880	2.784701	2.746503
Egypt	0.284416	2.774566	3.418432
El Salvador	0.439627	0.544251	0.435541
Ethiopia	0.186352	0.761277	0.494657
Fiji	0.323281	0.888106	0.704338
Finland	0.808155	0.533692	0.573808
France	1.247571	0.580828	0.541558
Germany	1.620924	0.593447	0.585385
Ghana	0.181388	0.594074	0.386978
Greece	0.487114	0.743621	0.735263
Guatemala	0.511509	0.469705	0.352328
Honduras	0.236993	0.619849	0.394077
Haiti	0.620852	0.723698	0.683331
Hong Kong	1.148382	0.540261	0.508282
Hungary	1.080037	0.878956	0.779493

Iceland	0.209668	0.728023	0.485188
India	0.694228	0.304014	0.250187
Indonesia	0.312776	1.989717	2.005426
Iraq	0.227811	4.819997	5.314853
Ireland	1.006058	0.706071	0.597347
Israel	1.089991	0.561809	0.515575
Italy	1.368548	0.480249	0.461098
Ivory Coast	0.333827	0.634888	0.451045
Jamaica	0.491832	0.660255	0.964197
Japan	3.190643	0.251333	0.237154
Congo	0.292854	1.286922	1.150984
Korea	1.051003	0.361383	0.358363
Kuwait	0.381894	5.065906	6.245257
Liberia	0.450793	0.659097	1.006164
Libya	0.257064	5.623624	7.333882
Malawi	0.210086	0.633294	0.299503
Malaysia	0.528576	1.152944	1.163494
Malta	0.846098	0.525571	0.495602
Mauritania	0.200795	1.650788	2.119897
Mauritius	1.000297	1.000354	1.000349
Mexico	0.298141	3.715023	4.060126
Morocco	0.707574	0.788365	0.787996
Nepal	0.193914	0.375939	0.256365
Netherlands	1.042038	1.059349	1.052346
Nicaragua	0.153623	1.048262	0.870926
Nigeria	0.238894	3.960244	4.471093
Norway	0.551915	2.046237	2.198988
Pakistan	0.274582	0.370322	0.288618
Panama	0.243969	0.807335	0.619838
Papua New Guinea	0.284298	0.672894	0.369644
Paraguay	0.447954	0.729629	0.487748
Peru	0.415777	1.501802	1.632591
Philippines	0.382155	0.458245	0.424375
Poland	1.311398	0.722123	0.725683
Portugal	0.696748	0.522928	0.508487
Rumania	0.821631	0.932579	0.793255
Rwanda	0.212983	0.840634	0.558451
Saudi Arabia	0.257615	5.649036	6.828708
Senegal	0.587175	1.234513	1.248459
Seychelles	0.274075	0.588776	0.289645
Sierra Leone	0.598825	1.212409	2.094001
Singapore	0.980487	1.000922	0.992834
South Africa	0.235586	1.478172	1.779684
Spain	0.987262	0.480634	0.465698
Sri Lanka	0.367437	0.736497	0.605077
Saint Vincent	0.219321	0.711801	0.393523
Sudan	0.560842	0.671742	0.265724

Sweden	1.165211	0.543956	0.561291
Switzerland	1.523309	0.753772	0.753573
Syrian Arab Republic	0.350562	1.882503	1.884686
Thailand	0.392818	0.452186	0.304141
Togo	0.291439	0.903547	0.549882
Tonga	0.254268	0.676087	0.349865
Trinidad and Tobago	0.476716	1.866536	1.941574
Turkey	0.369368	0.330624	0.222932
Uganda	0.182421	0.514712	0.266515
U.R.S.S.	0.941911	1.838774	2.376494
Cameroon	0.234172	1.403889	1.254252
Tanzania	0.191221	0.583639	0.387587
U.S.	1.367647	0.551994	0.480474
Uruguay	0.480176	0.284985	0.182436
U.K.	1.175899	1.145269	1.160734
Venezuela	0.245011	4.312668	5.016976
Yugoslavia	1.043607	0.517408	0.486514
Zaire	0.304321	1.095989	1.522621
Zambia	0.340112	0.835421	1.321061
Zimbabwe	0.245448	0.632634	0.589603

5.5.2 Country Classification

As pointed out earlier, regions within countries are rarely homogenous, but, rather, are highly heterogeneous. For example, in the United States, the northeast is highly industrialized, while the mid-west is highly resource-intensive. It therefore follows that, theoretically speaking, countries cannot be classified, outright, as being either *manufacturia*s or *primaria*s.

This having been said, one can nonetheless derive summary classifications of countries, based on aggregate (i.e. national) factor intensities. Such measures provide the basis for categorizing countries as either *manufacturia*s, hybrid *manufacturia-primaria*s, or *primaria*s. Tables 5.7, 5.8, and 5.9 provide the corresponding lists for the countries in our sample. *Manufacturia*s include Japan, Germany, Switzerland, Italy, the United States, France, the U.K., and Sweden. Not surprising, the G-6 all the countries figure in this list. As can be seen, these countries' exports are intensive in research and development and labor.

Hybrid *manufacturia-primaria*s include Belgium-Luxemburg, Asutria, Korea, Ireland, and Spain. *Primaria*s include Canada, Brazil, Australia, many South and Central American countries, and almost all the African countries.

Table 5.7
Manufacturias

Country	R&D	K/L	E/L
Japan	3.190644	0.251333	0.237154
Germany	1.620924	0.593447	0.585385
Switzerland	1.523309	0.753772	0.753573
Italy	1.368548	0.480249	0.461098
U.S.	1.367647	0.551994	0.480474
Czechoslovakia	1.353644	0.530379	0.496222
Poland	1.311398	0.722123	0.725683
France	1.247571	0.580828	0.541558
Algeria	1.197633	0.701748	0.694112
U.K.	1.175899	1.145269	1.160734
Sweden	1.165211	0.543956	0.561291
Hong Kong	1.148382	0.540261	0.508281

Table 5.8
Hybrid *Manufacturias-Primarias*

Country	R&D	K/L	E/L
Israel	1.089991	0.561809	0.515533
Belgium-Luxembourg	1.087999	0.806263	0.836124
Hungary	1.080037	0.878956	0.779493
Denmark	1.059866	0.470512	0.368508
Austria	1.059126	0.597491	0.644605
Korea	1.051003	0.361382	0.358363
Yugoslavia	1.043607	0.517408	0.486514
Netherlands	1.042038	1.059349	1.052346
Ireland	1.006058	0.706071	0.597347
Mauritius	1.000297	1.000354	1.000349
Spain	0.987262	0.480634	0.465698
Singapore	0.980487	1.000922	0.992834
USSR	0.941911	1.838774	2.376494

Table 5.9
Primarias

Country	R&D	K/L	E/L
Brazil	0.859222	0.414197	0.357569
Malta	0.846098	0.525571	0.495602
Rumania	0.821633	0.932579	0.793254
Finland	0.808155	0.533692	0.573808
Canada	0.769839	1.084426	1.149509
Morocco	0.707574	0.788365	0.787996
Bulgaria	0.705711	0.706609	0.521595
British Virgin Islands	0.705558	0.488519	0.416753
Portugal	0.696748	0.522928	0.508487
India	0.694228	0.304012	0.250187
Haiti	0.620852	0.723698	0.683334
Cyprus	0.599331	0.641494	0.531398
Sierra Leone	0.598822	1.212409	2.094001
Senegal	0.587175	1.234513	1.248459
Sudan	0.560842	0.671742	0.265724
Norway	0.551915	2.046234	2.198988
Malaysia	0.528576	1.152944	1.163494
Guatemala	0.511509	0.469705	0.352328
Jamaica	0.491865	0.660255	0.964197
Greece	0.487114	0.743621	0.735268
Uruguay	0.480176	0.284985	0.182436
Trinidad and Tobago	0.476716	1.866536	1.941574
Costa Rica	0.476247	0.753543	0.492964
Dominica	0.467396	0.971854	0.736985
Liberia	0.450793	0.659097	1.006164
Paraguay	0.447954	0.729629	0.487748
El Salvador	0.439627	0.544251	0.435541
Peru	0.415777	1.501802	1.632591
Thailand	0.392818	0.452186	0.304141
Philippines	0.382155	0.458245	0.424372
Kuwait	0.381894	5.065906	0.452517
Turkey	0.369368	0.330624	0.222932
Chile	0.367584	0.845901	1.255672
Sri Lanka	0.367437	0.736497	0.605077
Syrian Arab Republic	0.350562	1.882503	1.884686
Zambia	0.340112	0.835421	1.321061
Ivory Coast	0.333827	0.634888	0.451045
Fiji	0.323281	0.888106	0.704338
Dominical Republic	0.319279	0.521154	0.379522
Australia	0.316109	1.204025	1.309904
Indonesia	0.312776	1.989717	2.005426
Central Africa Rep.	0.311729	0.739121	0.594202
Zaire	0.304321	1.095989	1.522621
Mexico	0.298141	3.715023	4.060121
Congo	0.292854	1.286692	1.150984

Togo	0.291439	0.903547	0.549882
Chad	0.286149	0.482828	0.433555
Egypt	0.284416	2.774566	3.418433
Papua New Guinea	0.284298	0.672894	0.369644
Columbia	0.276779	0.734514	0.441065
Pakistan	0.274458	0.370322	0.288618
Seychelles	0.274075	0.588776	0.289645
Saudi Arabia	0.257615	5.649036	6.828708
Libya	0.257064	5.623624	7.333882
Tonga	0.254268	0.676087	0.349865
Argentina	0.254041	0.925586	0.685999
Zimbabwe	0.245448	0.632634	0.589603
Venezuela	0.245011	4.312668	5.016976
Panama	0.243969	0.807335	0.619838
Nigeria	0.238894	3.960244	4.471093
Belize	0.237553	0.545203	0.294494
Honduras	0.236993	0.619849	0.394077
South Africa	0.235586	1.478172	1.779684
Cameroon	0.234172	1.403889	1.254252
Cook Islands	0.229505	0.799291	0.421048
Iraq	0.227811	4.819997	5.314853
Benin	0.227708	0.962845	0.542161
Bangladesh	0.225636	0.290352	0.228108
Cuba	0.222552	0.470132	0.246174
Saint Vincent	0.219321	0.711801	0.393523
Burundi	0.213169	0.568461	0.278484
Rwanda	0.212298	0.844063	0.558451
Malawi	0.210086	0.633294	0.299503
Iceland	0.209668	0.728023	0.485188
Bolivia	0.204072	1.723181	2.327743
Mauritania	0.210079	1.650788	2.119897
Burma	0.195572	0.886165	0.554516
Nepal	0.193914	0.375939	0.254636
Tanzania	0.191221	0.583639	0.387587
Ethiopia	0.186352	0.761277	0.494657
Uganda	0.182421	0.514712	0.266515
Ecuador	0.138188	2.784701	2.746503
Ghana	0.181388	0.594074	0.386978
Nicaragua	0.153623	1.048262	0.870926
Afghanistan	0.139296	1.734469	1.553326

5.5.3 Horizontal Trade: The Evidence

It is well known that horizontal or intra-industry trade represents a significant portion of world trade. Some estimate that one quarter of world trade is intra-industry. In 1996, 57 percent of U.S. foreign trade took place within rather than across industries. European intra-industry trade stood at 60 percent. Japanese intra-industry trade, however, is considerably lower, at 20 percent.

This is borne out by the factor content data presented in Table 5.7. G-6 countries, with the exception of Japan, report R&D ratios (Column 1) that are close to unity, indicating the presence of R&D-intensive exports and imports (intra-industry trade). The United States, Germany, Italy, France, and Great Britain all report values between one and two, with most under 1.50. Japan, on the other hand, reports a value of 3.19. This, it could be argued, reflects the little intra-industry trade that is carried out in Japan.

5.6 Relationship to Existing Literature

These findings, I argue, are consistent with the results reported in the empirical trade literature, from Leontief (1953) to Bowen Leamer and Sviekauskas (1987). Starting with Leontief (1953), the results reported above show the United States to be a net exporter of labor and a net importer of capital, in keeping with the underlying nature of industrial trade. By the end of World War II, the United States had, owing to natural resource depletion, become a net importer of raw materials and transformed raw materials. Specifically, it had felled most of its forests in the mid-West and run down its stock of commercially-viable iron ore (Mesabi mines in Minnesota). Leontief's findings, while at odds with traditional Heckscher-Ohlin trade theory, are consistent with the model of vertical trade presented here. While the United States is well-endowed with capital, relative to its trading partners, its exports are nonetheless labor intensive.

Bowen, Leamer and Sviekauskas (1987) carried out what many consider to be the most extensive test of Heckscher-Ohlin-Vanek trade theory yet. As their results show, industrialized countries (*manufacurias*) such as France, Germany, Italy, Japan, Switzerland, and the United Kingdom are net importers of capital, and in general, net exporters of labor, while countries such as Argentina, Canada, Finland, are net exporters of capital, and net importers of labor.

5.7 Vertical Trade: Site Switching and U.S. Mineral Trade

In this section, I examine a case of site-switching, that of the U.S. economy in the post-WWII period. From 1958 to 1973, U.S. manufacturing value added increased at an average annual rate of 4.217 percent. Table 5.10, entitled Sources of Selected U.S. Mineral Supplies 1954–1977, illustrates the concept of site switching and its effect on U.S. foreign trade. For example, Columns 1 and 2 show U.S. domestic production and imports of refined zinc, expressed in percentage terms. In 1954, 82.7 percent of U.S. zinc came from domestic production, while 14.7 percent came from imports.[6] By 1977, only 44.7 percent came from domestic production, while imports accounted for 51.1 percent. Columns 3 and 4 show U.S. domestic production and imports of ferromanganese from 1960 to 1977. We see that like zinc, domestic production as a proportion of total domestic supply has decreased over this period. In 1960. domestic production accounted for 87.4 percent, with imports at 12.6 percent. By 1977, domestic production had fallen to 37.5 percent of overall supply, while imports had risen to 59.1 percent.

Like other empires before it, the United States will, according to the model presented above, be increasingly confronted with the problem of site exhaustion, which, in turn, will have important implications for international trade. As raw material sites are drawn down in the United States, U.S. companies, mostly multinationals, will turn to other countries in search of new sites. Owing to the corresponding capital and energy intensities, it stands to reason that, all other things being equal, U.S. imports will become increasingly capital intensive.

Table 5.10
Sources of Selected U.S. Mineral Supplies 1954–1977

Year	U.S. Zinc Production	U.S. Zinc Imports	U.S. Ferro Production	U.S. Ferro Imports
1954	74.3	14.7		
1958	76.3	19.1		
1962	79.9	12.9	86.1	13.9
1966	69.5	18.9	75.7	19.8
1970	72.2	21.4	74.3	25.7
1974	38.0	37.0	38.5	29.7
1977	37.2	51.1	37.5	59.1

Source: Fischman (1980), Chapter 4.

5.7.1 Growth Rates of Output and Trade

The presence of site exhaustion and site switching, I argue, makes for situations in which the rates of growth of a country's total output and industrial trade can differ markedly. The case of the U.S. steel industry in the post-WWII period is a case in point. Prior to 1950, U.S. steel mills imported their iron ore primarily from the Mesabi Iron Range in Northern Minnesota. The associated industrial trade was inter-regional in nature. Northern Minnesota exported iron ore to the Steel Belt, and imported finished products (e.g. automobiles). World War II, however, exacted a heavy toll on these deposits. By the late 1940's, extraction costs were rising as companies were forced to mine lower grades of ore. A rising $\lambda(t)$ eventually led U.S. steel companies to switch *primaria*'s, opting for Northern Quebec/Labrador, where large, rich iron ore deposits were known to exist. In 1955, Canadian exports of iron ore more than doubled going from 6,678 million metric tons to 14,772 million metric tons. In 1956, they increased to 20,273 million tons. Clearly, the presence of site switching goes a long way in explaining why the rate of growth of Canadian trade in the post-WWII period far exceeded the rate of growth of Canadian GNP.

Theoretically, for constant values of $\lambda(t)$, the rate of growth of *manufacturia-primaria* trade should mimic the rate of growth of *manufacturia-primaria* output. For example, if $v(t)$ grows at 3 percent per annum, then $m(t)$ should grow at 3 percent per annum. If, however, $\lambda(t)$ is not constant, but rather increases over time as the resource in *primaria* is depleted, then three situations may arise. First, if, to begin with, *manufacturia*'s industrial trade occurs with a *Primaria* within its national border, and if no other *primaria*'s exist within its borders, then growth may result in international site switching and a concommittant disproportionately high rate of growth of international trade. Second, if *manufacturia*'s industrial trade occurs with a *primaria* within its national border, and other *primaria*'s exist within its borders, then growth may result in infra-national site switching. One region declines while another prospers. In this case, international trade is unaffected. Third, if *manufacturia*'s industrial trade occurs with a foreign *primaria*, then growth will simply result in international substitution site switching, where foreign *primaria* is substituted for another.

As a general rule, the greater is the rate of growth of value added in *manufacturia*, the greater is the probability of site switching, and, hence, the greater is the probability that the rate of growth of international trade exceeds the rate of growth of overall economic activity.

The Rates of Growth of Trade and Output

It is a well accepted fact that the rate of growth of international trade in the post-WWII period has exceeded, by far, the rate of growth of output. Kenwood and Lougheed (1992) report that from 1948 to 1960, world trade increased from $53.300 billion to $112.300 billion, which corresponds to an average annual rate of growth of 6 percent. From 1960 to 1973, average growth rates of 8 percent per annum were recorded. However, with 1973 came the end of high growth rates.

From 1903 to 1979, the growth rate hovered around 4.5 percent; from 1980 to 1988, it fell further to 4 percent. According to Kenwood and Lougheed (1992), the volume of trade in the post-WWII period exceeded the increase in the volume of production:

Another important feature of world trade during this period was that, in almost every year, the increase in its volume of exceeded the increase in the volume of production. In other words, trade led economic growth. From 1953 to 1963, trade in primary products rose by 44 percent, and in manufactures by 83 percent. During the same years, agricultural output rose by 22 percent and mining and manufacturing output by 54 percent. despite the slowdown in trade and production after 1973, the same situation existed throughout the period 1963 to 1988 (Kenwood and Lougheed 1992, 286).

Post-WWII economic growth, it therefore follows, has given rise to a disproportionately high rate of trade growth. While some of this owes to the emergence of new industrialized nations such as Japan and Korea, there can be no doubt that a non-negligible part is the direct result of site-specific resource exhaustion and site switching. The Mesabi-Northern Quebec parable referred to above stands as a metaphor of post-WWII growth in output and trade.

5.8 Vertical and Horizontal Trade and Multinational Firms: The Evidence

As pointed out in the previous chapter, our model of vertical and horizontal trade makes a number of predictions regarding multinational firms. For example, vertical multinationals are typically highly-integrated (downstream) manufacturing firms which, when faced with the problem of site-exhaustion, turn to foreign sources. Horizontal multinationals, on the other hand, are manufacturing firms that, wanting to minimize differential spatially-related costs (tariffs, transportation costs), establish industrial entities in foreign countries. It follows that multinational source countries will, in general, be *manufacturias*, while host countries will, in general, be *primarias*. Referring to Table 5.11, we see that, in general, MNE source countries (net exporters of FDI) are R&D intensive, while host countries (net importers of FDI) are capital and energy intensive.

As pointed out in Chapter 4, the *primaria*-manufacuria model assumes perfect factor mobility across regions. Capital and labor can migrate from one region to another, as can technology, the latter by way of managerial transfers. Trade barriers, defined generally to include transport costs, tariffs, quotas (quantity restrictions), can, and in most cases will, result in foreign direct investment, where producers from one region will direct invest in another. Other causes of extra-region investment include what Raymond Vernon referred to as the technology gap, namely the existence of knowledge-based asymmetries. For example, the lack of managerial expertise in a *primaria* may result in upstream vertical investment by foreigners.

Table 5.11
Factor Intensities and Foreign Direct Investment: OECD Evidence

Country	R&D	K/L	E/L	Inflows	Outflows	Net
United States	1,367647	0,551993	0,480474	927378	876705	-50673
United Kingdom	1,175899	1,145268	1,160734	319726	566400	246674
Germany	1,620924	0,593446	0,585385	116467	422455	305988
France	1,247571	0,580828	0,541557	215804	347939	132035
Netherlands	1,042038	1,059349	1,052346	159523	250860	91337
Japan	3,190639	0,251332	0,237154	26008	248729	222720
Canada	0,769829	1,084425	1,149508	99000	120113	21113
Switzerland	1,523309	0,753772	0,753573	34680	119187	84506
Belgium	1,087999	0,806263	0,836119	123206	109350	-13856
Sweden	1,165210	0,543955	0,561291	127633	102114	-25519
Spain	0,987261	0,480634	0,465698	97780	93236	-4544
Italy	1,368548	0,480248	0,461098	37697	71148	3451
Finland	0,808155	0,533692	0,573808	22841	40760	17919
Denmark	1,059865	0,470512	0,368508	32176	32958	782
Korea	1,051003	0,361379	0,358363	24653	29018	4366
Norway	0,551915	2,046230	2,198988	26670	28131	1460
Ireland	1,006057	0,706071	0,597347	17451	26895	9444
Australia	0,316109	1,204025	1,309903	58910	26596	-32314
Austria	1,059125	0,597491	0,644605	21084	18155	-2929
Portugal	0,696747	0,522927	0,508486	17501	10463	-7038
Turkey	0,369368	0,330624	0,222932	8116	2087	-6029
Hungary	1,080037	0,878956	0,779492	19618	1261	-18357
Czechoslovakia	1,353644	0,530379	0,496220	15233	828	-14404
Poland	1,311397	0,722120	0,725683	30616	639	-29977
Greece	0,487114	0,743621	0,735260	26942	573	-26369
Iceland	0,209668	0,728023	0,485188	476	380	-9067
Mexico	0,298141	3,715020	4,060120	0	81570	-81570

5.9 Trade and Networks: The Evidence

To what extent does trade in general, and international trade in particular occur within the confines of well-defined networks? As a corollary, we could ask the following question, namely, to what extent does trade occur within traditionally-defined markets (arms-length)? In this section, we attempt to answer these questions. To begin with, we examine the literature on border effects. Border effects refer to the effect of geopolitical borders on trade activity, be it in terms of factors (Feldstein and Horioka 1980), or goods and services (McCallum 1995; Helliwell 1998). In traditional models of trade, geopolitical borders are assumed to be neutral in their effect on trade flows. Trade policy, on the other hand, is not. Tariffs, quotas, subsidies, etcetera, are assumed to affect the direction and magnitude (density) of trade.

5.9.1 Border Effects: Trade Flows

In 1995, John McCallum published a paper entitled "National Borders Matter: Canada-U.S. Regional Trade Patterns," in which he presented evidence of the existence of non-negligible border effects in Canada-U.S. trade. In short, McCallum showed that trade densities within Canadian provinces were as much as 14 times as great as those between Canadian provinces and comparable states in the United States. Once all other factors had been accounted for, borders appeared to have a greater than anticipated effect on trade flows. This was to mark the beginning of extensive research into border effects in merchandise trade.

Subsequent work showed that border effects were not specific to Canada-U.S. trade, but, instead, were ubiquitous. Shang-Jin Wei (1996) found evidence of non-negligible border effects in OECD countries. Specifically, he found that an average country imports about two and a half times as much from itself as from an otherwise identical foreign country, after controlling for sizes of exporter and importer, their direct distance, geographic positions relative to the rest of the world, and possible linguistic ties. John Helliwell (1998) showed that trade densities within developing countries were up to 50 or 100 greater than trade across national borders.

The evidence is unequivocal: national borders—and regional borders—affect trade, both in terms of its direction and magnitude. As a number of authors have pointed out, this can be attributed to a number of factors, including distance (market-separating effects), the presence of local networks, local norms, and uncertainty. According to John Helliwell:

> Because studies have found that policy barriers are not an important cause of the remaining border effects among the industrialized countries, the reason must lie elsewhere. I have long been convinced that the underlying explanation must be able to deal simultaneously with border effects and very large market-separating effects of distance. What happens to trade as distance grows, as borders are crossed, and as one moves from the known into the unknown, or at least the least familiar? Being further from home usually

means being less well-connected to local networks, less able to be sure how much to trust what people say. (Helliwell 2002, 14)

He adds:

> The core of my favorite explanation for border effects is that it is cheaper and easier to operate within networks of shared norms and trust, and the density of such networks declines with distance, and especially as one crosses national borders. (Helliwell 2002, 17)

What is particularly interesting to note is the extent to which border effects are related to the theory of neural networks as presented in Chapter 2. As Helliwell makes clear, the basic underlying problem is information. Local networks solve the problems of incomplete information and security of supply, via the corresponding institutions (legal, political, etcetera).

It would therefore stand to reason that by enlarging networks via the process of economic and geopolitical integration, border effects would diminish. Economic and geopolitical integration would result in larger networks, networks that would be trade enhancing. The evidence appears to support such a view. In his work on trade biases in OECD countries, Shang-Jin Wei found that the home bias in European Community countries was halved from 1982 to 1984. Similar results were found in the case of trade among NAFTA countries (Canada, U.S., and Mexico).

5.9.2 Foreign Direct Investment

Whereas the border effects literature points to the dominance of intra-network (geopolitical) over extra-network trade, one could argue that the presence of highly-integrated (vertically and horizontally) multinational firms points to the dominance of intra-firm trade over extra-firm trade. Multinational firms prefer the internal network that is the integrated firm, to the market (i.e. arms-length transactions). United Nations data show that roughly half of world trade originates in multinational firms, while roughly a third of world trade is intra-firm in nature. That is, occurs between subsidiaries of multinational firms. What is particularly interesting is the fact that intra-firm trade has risen over the last two decades. For example, the OCED reports that U.S. intra-firm trade as a share of all goods traded increased from 32.8 percent in 1990 to 36.2 percent in 1999. Japanese intra-firm trade as a share of all goods traded increased from 16.6 percent in 1990 to 30.8 percent in 1999.

5.10 Conclusions

International trade can be either vertical or horizontal in nature. Vertical trade is determined, in large measure, by the exigencies of production processes. Resource-rich regions produce and export intermediate goods, while R&D regions produce and export finished goods. Capital and labor move, although not perfectly, between *primarias* and *manufacturias*. Horizontal trade, on the other hand, is determined by a number of factors, including research and development and advertising.

The evidence is nonequivocal: trade flows, from ancient Sumer to modern-day Japan, have been determined, in large part, by the exigencies of industry. The result has been vertical trade, in which raw materials are traded against value added. Determining both the direction and nature of such trade flows are such things as resource deposits and transformation technology. Throughout the 19th century, Great Britain with its superior transformation technology, imported raw materials and exported value added. Throughout the 20th century, the United States, Japan, and Germany did likewise.

Capital and labor endowments, have little bearing on trade flows, as both have exhibited surprisingly high levels of mobility over time and space. Furthermore, the evidence also indicates that, as far as the institutions of trade are concerned, networks dominate markets, whether is be at the national level, or at the firm level. As the border effects literature shows, networks matter.

5.11 Appendix: The Measurement of Trade Flows

National and international agencies (United Nations, OECD, WTO) report trade flows in terms of the value of exports and imports, and in certain industries, the quantity of goods and services exported and imported. Nowhere are trade flows reported in terms of value added. It could be argued that if world trade was confined to trade in final goods (i.e. not requiring further transformation), then, this would not, as such, be a problem. If, however, trade in intermediate goods is significant, then measuring trade in terms of the total value of exports and imports raises a number of issues, not to say problems.[7]

Consider the following example. Suppose that a region—call it *primaria*—exports iron ore to a second region—call it *manufacturia*—which produces cold-rolled steel. Suppose that each dollar of cold-rolled steel consists of fifty cents worth of iron ore, and fifty cents worth of value added. *Primaria* exports fifty cents of iron ore to *manufacturia*, which transforms it into one dollar's worth of cold-rolled steel. *Primaria* then imports fifty cents of cold-rolled steel. Total world exports, in this case, would stand at one dollar. However, in actual fact, given that *primaria'*s imports contain twenty-five cents worth of iron ore, it stands to reason that, in actual fact, it is only importing twenty-five cents of value added from *manufacturia*, and, likewise, *manufacturia* is only importing twenty-five cents of iron ore from *primaria*. Twenty-five cents worth of iron ore is "cross-hauled" between *primaria* and *manufacturia*. The point is that trade in intermediate products biases upwards true trade flows. In this case, measured trade is two times as great as actual trade flows.

This result can be generalized as follows. Suppose that the production technology to produce good x consists of n separate sub-processes (e.g., raw materials, processing raw materials, part fabrication, assembly, painting, etcetera). Define m as the number of localizations (individual countries) at which different sub-processes are carried out. Also suppose that the value added at each location is simply $1/m$ of the total value added (i.e. price of the finished good). The extent to which measured trade is affected by the spatial distribution of production across countries is defined by Equation 5.1 where α is the scaling factor. If $m=1$, then there is no trade. If $m=2$, then the measured trade scaling factor is one.

For example, in the case above, for one dollar of final product, there will be one dollar of trade. If $m=4$, then the scaling factor rises to 2.25; if $m=8$, then it jumps to 4.375. Thus, for one dollar of output, there will be 4.375 dollars of measured trade.

$$\alpha = \frac{m^2 - m - 2}{2m}$$

(5.1)

Clearly, the current practice of measuring trade on the basis of export and import valuation, while suited for tariff purposes, is totally unsuited for analytical purposes. What is needed is a value added-based measurement of trade flows. As will be argued later, the recent manifold increase in world trade can, in large part, be attributed to the spatial dispersion of manufacturing activity, sometimes referred to as off-shore production. Manufacturing firms in Western industrialized countries have, over the past decade, moved parts production, and assembly off-shore, in search of higher returns. Actual trade has increased, but by far less than measured trade indicates.

$$\beta = \frac{m-1}{m}$$

(5.2)

The extent to which actual trade—as opposed to measured trade—increases in response to spatial dispersion is defined by Equation 5.2 where β defines the actual trade scaling factor. For the case in which $m=2$ actual trade is one-half, or fifty cents. For $m=4$, actual trade is seventy-five cents. As m and n tend towards infinity, β tends towards unity. Trade can never exceed total value added.

6

Trade Policy: A Network Approach

Since trade ignores national boundaries and the manufacturer insists on having the world as a market, the flag of his nation must follow him, and the doors of the nations which are closed against him must be battered down, Concessions obtained by financiers must be safeguarded by ministers of state, even if the sovereignty of unwilling nations be outraged in the process.

—Woodrow Wilson, 1907

6.1 Introduction

For over two centuries, the study of trade policy has, for the most part, been marred by ideology, notably by the ideology of free-trade. Anything short of complete free trade is seen as being sub-optimal, and, more importantly, welfare reducing. In other words, any form of government intervention is viewed as sub-optimal, and, as such, is to be avoided at all costs.

There are, of course, exceptions, such as the infant industry argument, and, more recently, strategic trade policy. While either can be used to rationalize intervention, each suffers from a number of problems. The infant industry argument, as an approach to trade policy, is incomplete, owing, in large measure, to the absence of a well-defined time framework. What is the optimal protection period? While human infants grow into adults in roughly 20 years, it is not known how much time is required for an industry to mature. Strategic trade policy suffers from the underlying game-theoretical implications, specifically of being a zero-sum game. Welfare gains are achieved at the expense of foreigners.

This has cast a pall on trade policy in general. In short, notwithstanding U.K. trade policy from 1846 on, and U.S. trade policy from 1934 on (Reciprocal Trade Agreements Act), according to this literature, politicians and governments

113

throughout the world have introduced trade legislation that has been welfare decreasing—that is, has harmed their constituents. Moreover, they have done so repeatedly despite having knowledge (from classical trade theory) of its sub-optimality.

The historical record is replete with what could be labeled trade-policy success stories. One hundred and fifty years of U.S. commercial policy contributed, at least indirectly, to the creation of the greatest industrial nation in the history of mankind. From a lowly colony, the United States went on to surpass its colonial master. Ibid for Germany and Japan, not to mention Great Britain prior to 1846. These facts, I argue, cannot and should not be ignored.

The network approach to industrial trade, I argue, provides a more balanced approach to the study of trade policy, one which is consistent with the historical and empirical record, and one that is less damning of roughly 7,000 years of trade policy. Industrial trade policy, I argue, is a common feature of all modern societies, and, more importantly, the embodiment of a number of species-specific traits, not the least of which is the desire on the part of Homo sapiens-sapiens to transform endowments of raw materials, using their energy and organization. Another is the desire to establish, be part of, and oversee one's own trade network; in short, not to be subordinate. Put differently, trade policy has been consistent with man's fundamental, underlying nature. Cast in terms of Abraham Maslow's "needs hierarchy," individuals and societies have lower-order and higher-order needs, networking and industrialization being higher-order needs.

Peoples have over the course of history—ancient and modern—sought to amass/create wealth and build empires. As the earth is finite in nature, it stands to reason that conflict would be endemic to the model—that is, conflict arising from empire building.

The network approach to trade, I argue, provides valuable insights into trade policy, both in the past and in the present. Industrial trade networks, as shall be shown here, change over time, depending on a number of factors, including growth, resource exhaustion, and, of course, technological change. They can be created, as was the Canadian federation in 1867 and the Soviet Union in the post-World War I period. Similarly, they can be dismantled, as were the Mercantile empires of the 17th and 18th century. They can expand, and they can contract. The Portuguese and Spanish empires are good examples. This chapter examines trade policy from a network point of view using a series of historical examples.

6.2 Trade Network Formation

It is generally assumed, in the literature on customs unions, that sovereign countries or regions will, of their own volition, enter into welfare-improving trade agreements. As it turns out, however, such a view is an incomplete account of trade network formation throughout history. Prior to the 20th century and the emergence of the League of Nations and the United Nations, non-European countries (territories) had little-to-no say in these matters. In the large majority of these cases, trade networks were imposed on peoples against their will. The Opium wars in China are a case in point. The Warsaw Pact in the post-World War II period is another. Military might has, for most of history, been the determining factor. When countries needed raw materials, ordinary and extraordinary measures were taken to secure them. The recent Gulf War, pitting the G-6 countries against Iraq, is a good example of this. Not wanting a repeat of the energy crises of the 1970's, the G-6 countries, led by the United States, declared war on Iraq, whose earlier invasion of neighboring Kuwait was nothing more than a poorly-disguised attempt at disciplining an OPEC cheater.

6.2.1 Bargaining and Trade Networks

This raises a number of policy-related questions, including the formation of trade networks themselves. Starting from the premise that regions/countries are free to enter or exit networks (agreements), the question becomes how are networks created? What are the relevant parameters? In this section, cooperative bargaining theory is used to examine the process of trade network formation.

We begin with the concept of bargaining power. While member countries (regions) are assumed to be equal, the historical record has shown, beyond all reasonable doubt, that they are not. In general, *manufacturias* have had more bargaining power than *primarias*. They have used this bargaining power to end relationships, and contract with new *primarias*. *Primarias*, on the other hand, have typically had less bargaining power.[1]

6.3 Shocks

As the historical record makes abundantly clear, trade networks are not immutable, but rather, are, over the medium term, highly malleable. Regions/countries are added while others are deleted. Historically, imperial powers have abandoned former colonies, Canada being the quintessential example. This raises the question why? What are the factors that determine the internal dynamics of trade networks? What leads a network to expand, bringing new regions/countries into the fold, so to speak? Here, three factors are considered, namely growth, technological change, and site exhaustion.

6.3.1 Growth

As pointed out in the previous chapter, growth in the center's (i.e. manufacturias) capacity (and hence need) to transform raw materials/intermediate goods will necessarily increase the demand for feedstocks. This, in combination with the fact that specific raw material deposits (*primarias*) are finite, can force changes on the trade network. Specifically, in cases in which existing *primarias* are confronted with the possibility of resource exhaustion, new sources of raw materials deposits will be sought out.

As growth of transformation (i.e. value added) is inexorably based on growth in energy consumption, capital and labor being organizational inputs, it follows that the chief cause of *manufacturia* output and productivity growth is energy consumption growth. This is not to say that capital and labor are not required, but rather that they are necessary, not sufficient conditions for growth. As such, energy deepening, whether by a more intensive use of existing energy sources, or the discovery of new energy sources, will, at least theoretically, be an important source of change in industrial trade networks.

6.3.2 Technological Change

By technological change, it is commonly understood, changes to the technique of production/transformation and/or changes to the product (value added). Output-increasing process innovations increase the demand for raw materials/intermediate products for the reasons outlined previously. Specifically, the rate of growth of manufacturing value added increases, increasing the demand for manufacturing feed-stocks, otherwise known as raw materials/intermediate products.

As I have argued elsewhere (Beaudreau 1998,1999), the prime sources of output-augmenting process-based technological change have been energy-based. Examples include the advent of the high-efficiency steam-engine, and the advent of the alternating-current, electrical induction motor. Both increased throughput rates greatly, resulting in the first and second industrial revolutions.

A good example of trade network-altering technological change is the British experience in the 18th century, specifically, the birth of the a national textiles industry. Prior to the spinning jenny and the steam engine, Great Britain's empire provided it with furs from Canada and other colonies to transform into garments, and various raw materials, including wood, to garnish the Royal navy. The industrial revolution, as it were, rendered this network redundant, as cotton became king. Unfortunately, however, it had, in 1776, lost its prime cotton-producing colony, the United States (thirteen colonies). One could argue that by the 1820's, Britain's trade network had become redundant, a vestige of another era. Animal hides were out, and cotton and silk were in.

6.3.3 Natural Resource Site Exhaustion

Another shock is resource exhaustion. Natural resources can be either renewable or non-renewable. In the latter case, the resource stock is fixed, and is run down over time. There comes a time, T, when the resource is depleted. That is, it is no longer economically viable to exploit the resource. Affecting T is the rate of extraction and the initial stock (see Equation 4.4 in Chapter 4).

In this case, the colonies in question become redundant, as they no longer contribute to overall wealth. Attempts will, as such, be made to find new deposits. The end result is an altered network. A good example of this is the case of the Mesabi range in northern Minnesota, which, for years, provided iron ore to the U.S. steel industry. By the end of World War II, all economically-viable deposits of iron ore had been exploited, with the result that the U.S. steel industry had to turn elsewhere. Elsewhere in this case was the province of Quebec, where they found abundant deposits of high-grade iron ore. The Iron Ore Company of Canada, a conglomerate founded by the major U.S. steel producers, was set up to mine and process the ore, and ship it to the United States for further processing.

6.3.4 Political Shocks

Another source of changes to trade networks are political shocks. The overthrow of a *primaria* government by rebel forces, for example, can conceivably lead to changes in its trading patterns, severing ties with one *manufacturia*, and establishing ties with another. Motivating such changes are a number of factors, including the internal distribution of wealth and the distribution of opportunity, not to mention internal political in-fighting.

Other shocks include the changing of governments, the result of a democratic election. An incoming government may choose to sever former trade ties in favor of new ties. That is, abandon a previous network in favor of another.

6.4 Case Studies

In the remainder of the chapter, I consider a number of case studies, chosen to highlight the role of networks in trade policy.

6.4.1 Export Taxes on Wool and British

Industrialization: A Trade Networks Approach It is well known that throughout the 19th century, England was the textiles capital of the world, exporting its fine cottons, linens and wools to the four corners of the earth. Born of the industrial revolution, specifically, of the application of steam power to spinning and weaving, the U.K. textile sector was a veritable engine of growth of the 19th century U.K. economy.

What is less known, however, are its origins. As it turns out, the U.K. textile industry was the result of a decision on the part of successive governments to impose export taxes on raw wool from Ireland and Scotland. Throughout the 14th, 15th, and 16th centuries, the U.K. sent its wool abroad for processing, specifically to Holland, which, at the time, was the textile center of Europe. Thus, prior to the imposition of an export tax, Britain, Scotland and Ireland were constituent parts of the Dutch trade network, assuming the role of *primaria*.

This did not sit particularly well with British nationals, who felt that the U.K. should process its own wool and linen. In short, this amounted to creating an internal trade network. Raw fibers from England, Scotland and Ireland would, hitherto, be processed in the United Kingdom. Making this possible were a number of factors, not the least of which was the relevant technology. Specifically, the weaving and spinning technology employed by the Dutch was, for all intents and purposes, free. That is, appropriable. In little time, the British were as adept at weaving and spinning as the Dutch.

6.4.2 The U.S. Civil War as an Industrial Network Trade Policy-Related Dispute

The imposition of an export tax on fibers by the British was a severe blow to the Dutch. Processing centers, as pointed out earlier, live and die by their feed-stocks. With no feed-stocks, processing industries are useless, to say the least. As it turns out, this same scenario would play itself out again, but this time, the U.K. would be on the receiving end.

The application of steam power to Arkwright's spinning jenny revolutionized the textiles industry, not to mention, industry in general (industrial revolution). Continuous-flow mass production of cottons, linens and wools, increased greatly the demand for the corresponding feed-stocks, forcing producers to import cotton, wool and linen from abroad. An important source of cotton for the mills of Manchester, Lancastershire, and other industrial centers, was the U.S. southern states. The continued growth of the U.K. textile industry, especially, the cotton sector, resulted in a marked increase in the demand for raw cotton. This was especially true in the 1840's and 1850's when high-pressure steam engines replaced atmospheric ones, resulting in a manifold increase in throughput rates. For the U.S. to meet this demand, new lands would have to be brought under cultivation (cotton). For new lands to be brought under cultivation, new states would have to be created, and, more importantly, they would have to be slave states, slaves being an important factor input. Increasing exports of cotton would imply, in the name of reciprocity, increasing imports of finished goods from England.

This did not sit particularly well with the North. From 1789 onwards, attempts had been made to constitute an internal trade network, the idea being that the southern and western states would export raw materials to the industrial northeast for processing. Waterwheel-driven factories in the New England states would transform raw materials into finished products. Francis Lowell's textile mill in the city that bears his name (Lowell, Massachusetts) is a case in point.

This, I argue, contributed to the hostilities which, in turn, led to the Civil War. Under the pretext of emancipation, the North, not wanting to be crowded out (i.e. by Great Britain), set its sights on the U.S. south, specifically, on the cost of cotton. By eliminating slavery, the cost of cotton would increase, thus contributing to worsening the terms of trade (i.e. U.S. South-England) for the South, and hopefully, a lessening of international trade, and an increase in interregional trade.[2]

In the end, the Civil War accomplished what it had set out to do. From 1860 on, exports of cotton to the U.K. were reduced to a trickle. U.S. raw cotton would, from then on, be processed in the factories of the North, resulting in two decades of unprecedented growth. From an organizational point of view, the Civil War, and its aftermath, the Post-Bellum period, signaled the end of the England-Southern States trade network. The South would, from then on, be forced to trade with the North, at less advantageous terms of trade.

One could go as far as arguing that the Civil War represented a coming of age of the U.S. geo-political economic trade network. By purging the young nation of Southern commercial interests favorable to free-trade (with the U.K.), it reaffirmed its status as a geo-political economic network. Territorial expansion, would, as such, serve the interests of the whole country, and not those of a particular region (i.e. the South).

6.4.3 The World Wars and Trade Networks: A Trade Network Interpretation

Thus far, it has been shown that trade and trade networks have, throughout history, been at the center of many a conflict, many a battle, and many a war. The need for material and/or energy feed-stocks, as I have shown, has pitted brothers, cousins, neighbors, and friends against each other. The "need for greed," one could argue, has fuelled many a conflict.

In this section, it is argued that these same factors were, in large measure, responsible for the first and second world wars, fought in 1914–1918, and 1939–1945, respectively. The stakes were relatively simple, and, more importantly, trade network related, namely the creation of a European industrial trade network by Germany. The advent of extremely-high throughput, electric power-based mass production in North America and Europe, altered the scale of production and, consequently, the need for feed-stocks. The United States was a case in point. At the turn of the century, its relative size made the transition to extremely-high throughput techniques easier than in Europe, where countries were relatively small.[3]

The following developments, I argue, contributed in a non-negligible way to the outbreak of hostilities in Europe both in 1914 and 1939. The first was the advent of a new power-drive technology, capable of increasing output manifold, and consequently, providing the wherewithal for firms (German) to serve all of Europe, not just individual countries. The second was Germany's lead over its European rivals in adopting these new techniques. From 1900 to 1930, Germany's production and consumption of electric power went from 1 billion kilowatt hours to 29.1 billion. By way of comparison, Great Britain's production and consumption went from 0.2 billion kwhs to 17.6 billion kwhs. The third was the emerging industrial trade network and its internal workings, namely its growing need for energy and raw materials.

Combine this with the fact that Europe at the time was dominated by two vestigial industrial trade networks in the form of Great Britain and France, and one gets, almost inevitably, conflict. Perhaps the best way to see this is in terms of tournaments. Technological change, being what it was at the time, set up a tournament in which only one of the three, Germany, Great Britain, and France, would win, which in this case consisted of controlling the resulting European industrial trade network. Germany's need for raw materials and energy (hydro-electric) from neighboring countries led it to invade and/or annex parts of Europe to its emerging network. While its motives were clearly economic, it couched its actions in notions of historical retribution, race, etcetera.

Obviously, this did not sit well with the two other industrial empires in Europe, Great Britain and France, who, again, under false pretexts, declared war on Germany. One was the assassination of Archduke Ferdinand in Sarajevo. Another was the German invasion of Czechoslovakia.

The first and second World Wars, I maintain, were, in essence, industrial trade network-based conflicts, pitting declining industrial trade empires Great Britain and France, against a rising economic power, Germany. This is not to say that other factors were not present (racism, etcetera), but rather that, as was the case in most other trade network conflicts, they were not the principle cause.

The Allies' true intentions were revealed after the Second War World in the form of the Morganthau Plan, which called for the dismantling of German industry and the transformation of imperialistic industrial Germany into an pastoral, agrarian society.

6.4.4 The Soviet Union as Vertical Network Trade Building

For all that has been said and written about the Soviet Union, one fact has escaped most observers, namely that it was, first and foremost, an attempt on the part of its founding fathers, to create an industrial trade network (empire) by fiat, paralleling the industrial trade empires of the ancient and then contemporary world. While trumpeted as a victory of workers over capitalist repression, it must not be forgotten that the Russian revolution was about industrialization and, as Lenin himself pointed out, electrification. In fact, one could argue that electricity is what sold the revolution to the people.

The Soviet industrial trade network can be easily understood in terms of the model of industrial trade presented in Chapter 4. Lagging behind virtually all other European nations, the Russian Soviet Republic would invest heavily in electric power generation, and transform raw materials (feed-stocks) from the four corners of the network. The other Soviet Republics would provide feed-stocks to the industrial heartland, and, in return, receive finished manufactured goods.

What is particularly interesting to note is the fact that prior to the Bolshevik revolution, Russia's bold attempt to enter the power age was well received in the United States, the birthplace of the power revolution. Distinguishing the U.S. from the U.S.S.R, was the chosen means to the common end, namely, a high throughput, industrial trade network. The U.S. chose private enterprise, while the Soviet Union chose central planning.

6.5 The Fall of the Iron Curtain as an Industrial Network Trade Policy Dispute

The fall of the iron curtain, I maintain, has less to do with ideology, and more to do with industrial network trade policy. Two factors, I argue, prompted what in essence, is a case of network realignment—that is, countries leaving the Warsaw pact, and joining other networks. The first is the failure of the Warsaw Pact to generate comparable levels of wealth to the West. The second is the renewed emphasis in the 1980's of creating a single European market, whose stated purpose was to increase the level and rate of growth of material wealth.

Put differently, the Soviet Union as an industrial trade network had lost its appeal, not to mention its luster, while a united Europe presented itself as an attractive alternative.

6.5.1 Canadian Confederation (1867) as Industrial Network Trade Building

As pointed out above, trade networks are dynamic in nature, changing over time. Membership is not a right. In some cases, regions/countries may join existing trade networks, and others may be excluded, *de jure* or *de facto*. As it turns out, this was the case of Canada in the mid-19th century. Specifically, the repeal of the Corn laws in England in 1846 signaled a fundamental change in Britain's trade intentions. Emphasis would now be placed on trade with the United States and the Baltic countries. Canada, having neither cotton nor a large domestic market, was of limited—if not, marginal—interest.

The end of imperial preference provoked an existential crisis of sorts in Upper and Lower Canada. A provider of raw materials to Great Britain for a century (since the Conquest in 1759), Canada's merchant class found itself in a bind, to put it mildly. With its traditional markets gone, it turned to the United States trade network, in search of an outlet for its raw materials. The result was the

Elgin-Marcy free-trade agreement of 1854, ushering in free trade in raw materials. Having been shunned by Great Britain, Canadian merchants turned to the United States.

The optimism was short lived as a trade-related incident involving Great Britain and the United States (i.e. the Civil War) put an end to free trade. The incident in question was Great Britain's move to free trade in combination with trade policy in the United States. Great Britain's textile mills, now powered by high-pressure steam engines, would require increasing supplies of raw cotton. The U.S. south was its prime supplier. However, for raw cotton production to increase, new territories would have to be brought into production. More to the point, as pointed out earlier, new states would have to be "slave states," as slave labor was essential to low-cost raw cotton. New England industrialists opposed the *de facto* creation of a trade network with Great Britain. U.K. textile producers were more cost efficient than their New England counterparts, owing largely to the advantages of steam over water as the relevant drive technology.

In little time, slavery became the issue. If slavery was abolished, then the cost of cotton would rise, thus turning the terms of trade with the U.K. against the South. The stakes were clearly great. If slavery survived and prospered, then the North would suffer. In fact, one could argue that its very existence as a manufacturing center hung in the balance. The Civil War, it turns out, set out to settle the matter once and for all.

As it turned out, Canada's alleged involvement in the war, on the side of the South—given its ties with Great Britain whose interests were clearly aligned with those of the South—led the U.S. government to revoke the free trade agreement, putting Canada back to square one. Lacking a market for its raw materials, it, taking its cue from U.S. trade policy (Henry Clay and the American System), opted to create an internal trade network, known as Confederation. The Quebec City-Windsor corridor would become Canada's *manufacturia*, while the Maritime provinces, Northern Quebec, Northern Ontario and the Western provinces would become Canada's *primaria*. High external tariffs and transportation subsidies were the policy tools chosen by the government of John A. MacDonald.

Success or Failure

The fathers of confederation's intentions were clear: create a Canadian trade network not unlike that of their neighbors to the South. This raises a number of questions, notably, were they successful? Did Canada rival the United States?

The answer is no, and the reasons are as follows. While the U.S. had little need for Canadian raw materials in the 1860's, by the end of the century, things had changed. Raw materials, especially wood, had become more scarce, especially in the northern Michigan-Wisconsin-Minnesota area. This led U.S. venture capitalists to turn to Canada, and its abundant supply of raw materials, conveniently located at its doorstep. In short, the need existed to expand the internal-to-the United States trade network to include Canada. In little time, Canada's resource sector was under foreign—read: United States—control. The arrival, some twenty years later, of U.S. horizontal multinationals (Singer, Ford, General Motors, General Electric, Westinghouse) de facto put an end to the Canadian dream of a home-grown trade network.

Throughout much of the 20th century, Canadian trade policy was dualistic in nature. On the one hand, Canadian nationalists continued to push for a made-in-Canada trade network. Subsidies and trade restrictions on manufactured goods were the cornerstones of this policy. On the other hand, the Canadian economy continued to be drawn into the U.S. trade network. Raw material exhaustion in the United States, combined with the presence of U.S. foreign multinationals, increased cross-border trade in goods, services, and knowledge.

6.5.2 FTA and NAFTA as Industrial Network Trade Realignment

Canada's dichotomous trade policy, based on partial integration into the U.S. industrial trade network, and a domestic industrial trade network underwent a complete overhaul in the late 1980's with the signing of the Free Trade Agreement (1987), which removed remaining trade barriers with the United States. In this section, I examine the underlying causes of this paradigm shift in policy, as far as Canada was concerned. Why did a country, settled by French and British colonists, having chosen in 1867 to create a national trade network (National Policy of 1879), opt for free trade with the United States? Further, why did the United States, which, for a century, had opposed free trade with Canada, instigate the negotiations?

The principal cause, I argue, was the energy crises of the 1970's. The OPEC-induced oil embargoes (1973 and 1979) did two things. First, they cut off supplies of crude petroleum to the West. Second, they led to increased energy prices, which, as I have argued in earlier work (Beaudreau 1995,1998) reduced the rate of growth of energy consumption (energy deepening), which was one of the principal factors in the growth and productivity slowdowns of the 1980's and 1990's. Growth rates in Western industrialized democracies were more than halved; productivity growth rates were flat throughout this period (Madisson 1987).

After three decades (1945–1975) of steady output and productivity growth, governments were confronted with the specter of the steady-state, anathema to the western way of thinking. Output and productivity, it seemed would grow at considerably lower rates. Not surprisingly, they reacted, the U.S. government taking the lead. Faced with increased energy-supply insecurity, the U.S. administration turned to Canada, as it had at the turn of the century for wood fiber, and, at the end of World War II for iron ore. Canada had abundant supplies of oil and gas. The problem, however, was that Canada's National Energy Policy (NEP), put in place by the last of Canada's empire builders, former prime minister Pierre Trudeau. Aimed at restricting access to Canada's oil patch, specifically Americans, the NEP prompted the U.S. administration to conduct high-level talks with the Canadian government, led by Conservative Brian Mulroney.

The U.S.'s motives were clearly resource- and energy-related. Cheap Canadian natural gas would fire electric power plants throughout the industrial northeast. Canadian crude oil would flow south, and, in the event of renewed political instability in the Mid-East, would ensure supplies. Canada and Canadians were more ambivalent, reflecting its/their aforementioned dichotomous trade policy. Believers in a Canadian industrial trade network, with home-grown manufacturing firms transforming, using its abundant energy supplies, its abundant supply of natural resources. Canadians in raw material-exporting regions of the country, like their Confederate counterparts in the mid-19th century, favored free-trade with the U.S. Quebec and the Western provinces voted massively for free trade, while Ontario, the heart of the Canadian *manufacturia* voted resoundingly against it.

To convince the skeptics, the Canadian government established the MacDonald Commission, with a mandate to examine the underlying weaknesses of the Canadian economy (read: productivity and growth slowdown). The commission concluded that Canada's poor economic performance, especially in manufacturing, was to due to its failure to exploit economies of scale. This, in turn, was attributed to the small Canadian market, which limited production runs and hence increased costs. For over three decades, at a time when optimal plant size increased radically (post-World War II period), the small domestic Canadian market had not been an obstacle to high output and productivity growth; however, suddenly, it had become public energy number one.

The Free Trade Agreement was ratified in 1989. The FTA marked the end, so to speak, of a dream, the dream of a Canadian industrial trade network. Today, Canada and Mexico (under NAFTA) are members in good standing of the U.S.-based and controlled North American industrial trade network. Canada's *manu-*

facturia and *primaria* have since fallen under increased U.S. control, as have Mexico's. In many large corporations, regions of Canada and Mexico have been integrated into existing U.S. sales regions: British Columbia is part of the Pacific Northwest; Ontario is part of the Mid-East, and Quebec a part of New England.

Clearly, geographic borders matter little. What matters are the borders of the relevant industrial trade network, in this case Canada, the United States, and Mexico. That Canada and the United States do two billion dollars worth of trade each day is as revealing as California doing three billion dollars worth of trade daily with the other forty-nine states.

6.5.3 Japanese Industrial Network Trade

The Japanese experience since the restoration of the Meiji Dynasty is a good example of industrial network trade building.[4] An energy and resource-poor country, Japan has had to rely on its research and development (technology, know-how).

According to Mao-Tse Tung:

> As we all know, for nearly a hundred years China has been a semi-colonial country jointly dominated by several imperialist powers. Owing to the Chinese people's struggle against imperialism and to conflicts among the imperialist powers, China has been able to retain a semi-independent status. For a time World War I gave Japanese imperialism the opportunity of dominating China exclusively. But the treaty surrendering China to Japan, the Twenty-One Demands signed by Yuan Shih-kai, the arch-traitor of that time, was inevitably rendered null and void as a result of the Chinese people's fight against Japanese imperialism and of the intervention by other imperialist powers. In 1922 at the Washington Nine-Power Conference called by the United States. A treaty was signed which once again placed China under the joint domination of several imperialist powers. But before long the situation changed again. The Incident of September 18, 1931, began the present stage of Japan's colonization of China. As Japanese aggression was temporarily limited to the four northeastern provinces, some people felt that the Japanese imperialists would probably advance no farther. Today things are different. The Japanese imperialists have already shown their intention of penetrating south of the Great Wall and occupying all China. Now they want to convert the whole of China from a semi-colony shared by several imperialist powers into a colony monopolized by Japan. The recent Eastern Hopei Incident and diplomatic talks are clear indications of this trend of events which threatens the survival of the whole Chinese people. This faces all classes and political groups in China with

the question of what to do. Resist? Surrender? Or vacillate between the two? (Mao Tse-Tung 1935)

To be successful, it would have to transform intermediate inputs (transformed raw materials) better than its rivals. This, as it turns out, is what it set out to do. By focusing its efforts on quality and cost, Japanese manufacturers built a commercial empire, which is second to the United States. They did this by importing transformed raw materials from Australia, Canada, and South America, to name a few, and transforming them in cities like Kobe, Tokyo, Yokohama. The underlying principles were simple: Japan would import raw materials and export value added (transformation). This has become known as the Japanese model. The one important difference, however, is that unlike other Industrial Network Trade building nations (e.g. U.K., U.S.), Japan targeted the United States, a rival trade network, as its principal market, not the countries which supplied the raw materials.[5] In the 19th century, Britain exported its manufactures to markets in countries which supplied raw materials. The Japanese, however, targeted the U.S. market.

The reason, I argue, owes to the second spontaneous private market impossibility theorem, namely that there are no private incentives for individual producers to create markets (income). By targeting a rich, established market, Japanese manufacturers were able to circumvent this problem. That is, they were not required to "make the market" so to speak.

These two factors, I believe, are crucial to understanding the longstanding U.S.-Japan trade dispute. First, Japan, fully aware of the underlying causes of its success(es), has refused to open its market to U.S. manufactures. As many a Japanese trade official has proclaimed, Japan is a resource and energy-poor country which depends on manufacturing. Opening its market up to U.S. manufactures would be economic *hari-kiri*, as it would compromise its ability to import raw materials.

Another way to look at this is in terms of Industrial Trade Networks. In an ideal world, the U.S. and Japanese industrial trade networks would be independent entities, each having their own suppliers of raw materials, and each having their own markets. The problem, as far as the U.S.-Japan case is concerned, is the fact that Japan is a major player in a foreign industrial trade network. Japan exports manufactures to the U.S., but refuses to import them. U.S. exports to Japan are largely raw material based. However, letting U.S. manufactures into Japan might spell the end of Japanese manufacturing, given its dwindling knowledge-based advantage. Should this materialize, then Japan would, quite possibly, become part of the U.S. global industrial trade network.

6.5.4 The Crusades as a Network Trade Policy Dispute

As odd as it may sound, it could be argued, quite convincingly, that the Crusades were first and foremost about trade. While it is generally argued that religion, namely the Ottoman's occupation of Constantinople and Jerusalem, was the chief cause, a more careful examination seems to suggest otherwise. It must be remembered that in addition to spreading Islam, the Ottomans (Turks) were skilled traders, having established a vast trade network in what was formally the Byzantine empire and Asia Minor.

By launching the crusades, the West signaled their intention to limit or curtail Ottoman expansionism, and in the process, hopefully, regain some—if not all—the trading routes. Religion was, at best, a pretext, a rallying cry. What is particularly interesting, and, in my view, very revealing, is the fact that after having liberated Jerusalem, the Crusaders did not return home, but rather set up a series of trading posts that, over the course of the next two centuries, conducted trade with the West.

6.5.5 Free Trade as Global Industrial Network Trade Building

The argument here is simple, namely that over the past two hundred years, throughput rates in manufacturing have increased monotonically, with the result that today, a small number of plants (firms) can, at least theoretically, supply world demand. It therefore follows that from a social welfare point of view (i.e. minimizing costs), national markets should be replaced by one single global market. Take, for example, the case of Microsoft Corporation of Redmond, Washington, which could, conceivably, supply the world market for operating software from one location.

As argued earlier, free trade, as defined by 19th century British political economists, was an attempt at creating a single, global market, one having a small number of firms/plants, localized in Great Britain. In their words, Great Britain would become the workshop of the world. Their reasoning was, in general, sound. The steam engine had increased throughput rates such that, as far as textiles were concerned, the mills of Lancastershire and Manchester could in fact supply the world market.

Halevy described Ricardo as the theorist of 'the great English manufacturers, who dreamt of making the economic conquest of the world.' The weapon which the would-be conquerors intented to employ was an international free trade, justified by the doctrine of comparative advantage; the form of this projected economic dominance was to be a trading system established upon England's leading position in industrial production....The view that a freer trade would facilitate the perpetuation of England's industrial dominance was foreshadowed, in a mid-eighteenth-century debate, by Josiah Tucker, a mercantilist, who had become convinced that free-trade was in the British national interest. Tucker's arguments studded the parliamentary speeches in the discussions of Pitt's trade proposals in the eighties. We can follow the development of these ideas in the writings of James Mill, Robert Torrens (whose vision of trade-empire in 1815 was virtually an 'ideal-type' of free-trade mercantilism), David Ricardo, and Edward Gibbon Wakefield, among others. That this substantially mercantilist goal of making England the Workshop of the World, a goal largely set by the economists, was widely accepted, is apparent in surveying the parliamentary debates which led to the abolition of the corn laws, in the course of which Joseph Hume, and finally Sir Robert Peel made themselves its leading spokesmen. (Semmel 1970, 9)

As pointed out earlier, throughout the 19th century, the United States, fully aware of Britain's industrial might and imperialistic intentions, thwarted any and all attempts at free trade. U.S. industrialists, aware of the advantages of steam power over hydraulic power, sponsored trade bill after trade bill, the purpose of which was to prevent U.K. textiles and finished goods from gaining access to the growing U.S. market. Free global industrial network trade was out of the question, for obvious reasons. U.S. textile manufacturers were no match for their U.K. counterparts. U.S. trade policy fostered the creation of a U.S. industrial network, with the North as *manufacturia*, and the South and West as *primaria*. Trade was, however, encouraged.

A century later, the tables had turned. Owing in large measure to the new power drive source which was electricity, U.S. manufacturers enjoyed a significant advantage over their U.K. rivals, who were slow to convert to the new technology. By the 1930s, U.S. firms, giant in scope, dominated their European rivals, both cost-wise and product-wise. By the end of World War II, the U.S. had shed its protectionist past, and embraced free trade, knowing full well that no one, not England, France, or Germany, could compete with its industry.

Free trade became a virtue. The nation that had drafted the most repressive trade bill in world history, the Smoot-Hawley Trade Act of 1930, was now defending the virtues of free trade. Not everybody agreed. Other industrialized nations (Japan, Germany, France, England), with designs on strengthening their industrial trade networks, resisted. While paying lip service to free trade, Japan remained a protectionist nation. European nations, aware of the advantages of high-throughput production processes, moved towards unification, and, consequently, a single European industrial trade network, one whose size could rival the United States. The result is what trade economists refer to as trade blocs, but which, in reality, are industrial trade networks, in which resources and energy are traded for transformation.

6.6 On Motives and Masks

By this point in time, the reader will undoubtedly be somewhat wary of what appears to be a simplistic rationale for the events described above, namely "It's all about trade." Some will point out that the Civil War in the United States was not about trade, but about human rights, notably the rights of slaves. Others will argue that the Crusades were not about trade, but religion. More recently, one could argue that the Gulf War in 1991 was not about oil, but about international law, as set out by the United Nations charter. This raises a number of questions, namely, who's right? Is war fought over trade, or is it fought over ideals? Is it fought over what Carl Rogers refers to as basic needs, or is it fought over higher order needs (e.g. liberty, freedom, equality)?

Indeed, this is a difficult question, one historians have grappled with over for centuries. How to disentangle cause from effect, casual relationships from causal relationships? I do not profess to be in a position to provide definitive answers to this question. However, I would venture to argue that, on the basis of the evidence presented above, wealth creation/appropriation via the establishing and maintaining of industrial trade networks ranks among the leading rationales for human conflict. How then are we to understand the higher-order need rationales (i.e. the ones typically invoked)? Why tell the world that you are fighting a war against slavery, when, in actual fact, you are fighting to either maintain or increase material wealth? The answer, I believe, lies in our nature as a moral species. Unlike lower-order primates, we as a species are moral beings, with fully-developed consciences. To kill someone to appropriate their wealth is, in all codes of conduct, immoral. Further, it is hard—if not impossible—to convince a human being to sacrifice his/her life in the name of another person's wealth. Life is, in general, perceived of to be more important than material wealth.

Morality can, however, be co-opted into the service of material wealth appropriation. Homo sapiens-sapiens have, over the course of the last 300,000 years, used morality as a means to a baser game, namely material wealth appropriation.

In general, this has been done by pitting one set of moral values against another. In the case of the civil war, what was a trade network conflict was couched in moral terms, namely the desire on the part of the Northerners to abolish slavery, and extend the full slate of human and civil rights to Afro-Americans.[6] Being moralistic beings, we will (are prepared to) fight for principles. Among the latter are freedom, equality, the right to happiness, etcetera.

6.7 Conclusions

As I have attempted to demonstrate in this chapter, trade policy, the bane of classical and neoclassical economics, has been, and undoubtedly, will continue to be welfare increasing. As long as countries like Brazil aspire to building vertical trade networks, trade policy will continue to be the preferred tool. As long as Homo sapiens-sapiens as a species longs to do more than draw water and hew wood, trade policy will continue to play an important role in a country's political identity.

Clearly, trade policy is a thorn in the side of dominant nations (U.S., Europe). As they rely, increasingly, on imported raw materials and energy, attempts by feedstock nations to forge vertical trade networks of their own, will be frowned upon, if not openly discouraged. Yet the historical record is clear on this point: nations gain in resisting calls for free trade. The quintessential example is the United States, which throughout the 19th century, resisted any and all attempts by Great Britain to eliminate its trade restrictions. A little-known fact is that Great Britain had paid lobbyists in Washington throughout the 19th century, whose single purpose was to sell free trade. Had they been successful, there is every reason to believe that the United States would not be the dominant force it is today, but, instead, would be something not unlike Canada. In conclusion, the proposition that trade restrictions impede growth and development is, historically speaking, simply not true, at least not in general.

7

Trade and Networks: Implications and Consequences

7.1 Introduction

The findings of Chapters 1–6 have important implications for the study of international economics, not to mention the study of economics in general. Among these is the role of networks in large-scale—and small-scale—exchange. Networks and the associated public choice mechanisms have, since time immemorial, played a pivotal role in large-scale specialization and exchange. As the historical record makes abundantly clear, corroborated by the first and second private spontaneous market impossibility theorems, organized, large-scale trade requires government. The notion of spontaneous large-scale exchange (large-scale markets), the cornerstone of contemporary political economy, has no basis in history (ancient and modern), nor in theory. This raises a number of important methodological issues. For example, if networks and public choice are necessary conditions for the emergence of markets, why has political economy, the purported "science of wealth," been devoid of both? Why is it that, despite overwhelming evidence of the fundamental role of networks and government in the conduct of large-scale trade, 19th century political economists cast the nascent science of wealth (economics) in purely atomistic, individualistic terms? Why were the roles of government as "makers of markets" and "providers of exchange media," ignored? Why was the emphasis on "free" markets? Why was most of the analysis cast in real, not nominal terms?

In this chapter, I examine these questions. It will be argued that answers to these questions can be found in the very nature of 19th century political economy, namely as largely ideological, having little-to-no basis in science—or the scientific method. More to the point, late 18th century and 19th-century political economy was guided by one overriding principle, namely weakening (lessening) the role of the state (landowners) in the economic affairs of the nation, and strengthening the role of private agents, mostly merchants. Put succinctly, merchants, including private entrepreneurs, were more adept at creating wealth than were monarchs. Such was the gist of the single, most influential work of this period, namely Adam Smith's *An Inquiry into the Nature and Causes of the Wealth of Nations* published in 1776. According to Smith, industry, particularly steam-engine driven industry, was the prime source of the wealth of nations, not mercantilism, which he saw as a zero-sum game.

It is important to appreciate the context in which Smith and his continental collaborators, the French Physiocrats, found themselves, namely one whose institutional origins dated back to ancient Sumer, namely mercantilism. The 18th century mind was, in essence, the product of the Roman empire, steeped in classical though and institutions. Accordingly, government was synonymous with civilization, and, consequently, with large-scale exchange. John Law's Compagnie d'Occident is a case in point. Moreover, government, in the eyes of many, including Smith, was corrupt and inert which, in the presence of technological change (the steam engine), led to an intellectual call to arms. No holds were to be barred. A new ideology was needed, one which stressed the virtues of free,—in the sense of "free" of government—markets. Trade would heretofore be devoid of government. Private merchants (agents) would replace royal merchants. Reactions to the perceived-of inertness of government in the face of technological change ranged from country to country. France, for example, entertained the idea of constituting a class of scientists and engineers, whose task would consist of closing the technology gap with Great Britain. The leading protagonist, in this case, was Claude de Rouvroy, Comte de Saint-Simon.

The end result was a body of literature (i.e. political economy) that extolled the virtues of free markets, and condemned all things governmental and mercantile.[1] The point, however, is that no attempt was made to understand government, its function, its history, its development, and its raison d'être. That government was as old (ancient) as civilization was simply ignored.

The absence of a positive theory of government, combined with the ideological imperative that was classical political economy from Adam Smith to Alfred Marshall, weighed heavily in the balance. Spontaneous models of exchange, devoid of government, soon became the norm. Suggestions that free markets were not adept at solving coordination problems (underconsumption, overproduction) were decried, and denounced, often times with missionary zeal. Jean-

Baptiste Say's "Law of Markets" stands as a testimony to the religious fervor of early political economy.

The problem, however, is that Smith, Ricardo and Say threw the baby out with the bath water. While governments—in this case, monarchs—were indeed guilty as charged (e.g. corruption, largesse, inertia), the fact remained that they had been, were, and would continue to be a necessary condition for large-scale exchange (i.e. economic organization). Put differently, the coordination failures that underlie large-scale exchange could not be assumed away, or, for that matter, ignored.

Public choice and networks, as I have shown, are the *sine quo non* of large-scale exchange activity, and, consequently, of civilization. Spontaneous large-scale specialization exchange is, theoretically speaking, impossible. This is not to say that all things governmental are, by definition, Pareto improving. To do so would be pure folly, for obvious reasons. Clearly, governments can be a number of things, including excessive, inert, totalitarian, etcetera.

7.2 Implications for International Trade

Trade theory can be likened to a Greek tragedy, written in two parts. The first dates back to the early 19th century, and is synonymous with the names of David Ricardo and Henry Torrens, while the second dates back to the 1930's and is synonymous with two Scandinavian economists, Eli Heckscher and Bertil Ohlin. In keeping with science as practiced in the Renaissance, one would have thought that early "trade theorists" would have, above all else, set out to explain trade flows—that is, why commodities are exported and imported. Had they done so, there is little doubt that the outcome would have been different, and would have involved, in one form or another, networks. The reason is simple, namely that by the end of the 19th century, all trade occurred within well-defined mercantile networks. Had they chosen to study trade from a historical point of view—including ancient history—then, once again, networks would have played a prominent role.

Clearly, there was nothing scientific about early trade theory. In fact, one could argue that early trade theory was, as was most of 19th-century political economy, a form of social engineering, based on the poorly-defined notion of "freedom." That is, what if markets were "free." What if all bounties, taxes, and other trade restrictions were removed? What if taxes were abolished, or reduced substantially?

While there is nothing inherently wrong with counter-factual analysis—in fact, given the right circumstances, it can be highly insightful—19th century political economists were ill-prepared to raise such issues, the main reason being their poor—if not altogether non-existent—knowledge of history/institutions. For example, to properly frame the question of abolishing government, one must first ask oneself why government—and all other similar forms of governance—exists or existed to begin with? In other words one must have a theory of government that is sufficiently general so as to be able to handle both cases. As shown in Chapter 2, government and economic civilization are, historically speaking, collinear.

To advocate free trade—that is, trade free of all forms of government—is to ignore the important role government played in the rise of large-scale specialization and exchange. Put differently, markets were never free (of government), and more importantly, freedom in the sense of the n-person Nash game described in Chapter 2 is synonymous with no markets at all (i.e. inertia).

Early trade theory should, as such, be seen for what it was, namely an attempt at redrawing the U.K.'s industrial trade network. Trade had to be freed from the shackles of 18th century mercantilism, and updated—brought into line with the new reality that was early 19th century Great Britain. As Bernard Semmel noted:

> But what of the "science" of political economy itself? How "scientific" was, for example, its defense of free trade? List and Carey, and their followers, of course, charged that the devotion of the classical economists to an international free trade was grounded in their interest, as Englishmen, in keeping the rest of the world occupied in subordinate pursuits—mere hewers of wood and drawers of water for an industrial England. (Semmel 1970, 207)

The point is that classical trade theory should be seen for what it was, namely as an attempt by British political economists to realign the U.K.'s industrial trade network, away from its former colonies, over to new colonies rich in arable land—the source of food and cotton. Rape and plunder, as a means of acquiring scarce raw materials, was to be replaced by free trade. The terms of trade, skewed in favor of the *plunderer*—against the *plunderee*—would heretofore be determined by an "impartial" market. In short, free trade was an attempt by the British to redefine trade networks, away from costly geopolitical-economic entities over to pure economic entities.

Such was the theory. In practice, Great Britain (merchants and governments) proved itself to be as rapacious in its foreign policy as all other imperial powers, declaring war on a number of sovereign countries (e.g. The Opium Wars). Trade was not free, but, instead, was carried out under the auspices of chartered trading companies such as the East India Company, each constituting a government-sanctioned monopoly. Great Britain maintained settlements and concessions in Tientsin, Shanghai and Wei Hai Wei, China). What's more, Great Britain continued to pursue aggressively, commercial policy, most notably the United States, its former colony whose commercial value had skyrocketed. Cotton (abundant) from the U.S. south, as it turns out, was a highly coveted commodity in 19th century Great Britain.

Throughout the 19th century, trade theory remained unchanged. While it had been demonstrated, beyond a shadow of a doubt, that free trade was superior to autarky, virtually every western industrialized nation—Great Britain notwithstanding—adopted policies designed to protect (read: close) its domestic market—from the British. The United States and Germany are two cases in point. Important trade barriers were erected in 19th century Germany and United States, designed to foster manufacturing activity. Clearly, the Germans and the Americans were not prepared to let Great Britain monopolize manufacturing activity in the world, as it had so deftly planned. According to Frederich List:

> In the economical development of nations by means of external trade, four periods must be distinguished. In the first, agriculture is encouraged by the importation of manufactured articles, and by the exportation of its own products; in the second, manufacturers begin to increase at home, whilst the importation of foreign manufactures to some extent continues; in the third, home manufactures mainly supply domestic consumption and the internal markets; finally, in the fourth, we see the exportation upon a large scale of manufactured products, and the importation of raw materials and agricultural products.
>
> The system of import duties being considered as a mode of assisting the economical development of a nation, by regulating its external trade, must constantly take as a rule the principle of the industrial education of the country. (List 1856, 69)

World trade flows in the 19th century revealed, beyond a doubt, that something other than ratios of the average productivity of labor was at work, determining the gains from trade. Clearly, the factor content of trade, specifically, resources and value added, played an important role in determining trade flows.

This was brought to the attention of the economics profession by Scandinavian political economist Eli Heckscher, whose Ph.D. thesis consisted of a history of mercantilism. One could argue that anyone with a basic understanding of the history of mercantilism (empires) would know that endowments, especially of raw materials, are crucial to understanding trade flows. Ricardian trade theory, however, ignored endowments and eight thousand years of foreign trade, preferring to cast trade in terms of productivity-based comparative advantage.

In hindsight, it is not altogether surprising that an endowments-based theory of international trade would originate in Sweden, a country which, throughout its history, has served as source of raw materials for foreign powers. In many regards, Heckscher and his student, Bertil Ohlin's work on endowments is analogous to Canadian economist Harold Innis's "Staples" theory of international trade and development, which, as its name implies, is based on raw materials, specifically, exports of raw materials to industrialized countries.[2]

One could go so far as to argue that trade theory maps—in the mathematical sense—into the nature of the author's countries exports. Ricardian trade theory is based on transformation, transformation being Great Britain's comparative advantage in the 19th century. Eli Heckscher, Bertil Ohlin, and Harold Innis' writings on trade were based on endowments, endowments determining Sweden and Canada's comparative advantage. In short, both transformation-based and endowment-based theories of international trade are parts of a bigger whole, namely the theory of industrial network trade.

The story of what has come to be referred to as Heckscher-Ohlin-Samuelson trade theory reads, in many regards, like that of Ricardian trade theory, namely as being politically motivated. With the signing of the Reciprocal Trade Agreements Act in 1934, the Roosevelt government put the U.S. economy on a fast track to free trade, thereby reversing over a century and a half of restrictive trade measures, culminating in the Fordney-McCumber Tariff Act of 1922 and the Smoot-Hawley Tariff Act of 1930. Like Great Britain a century earlier, the United States now towered above its rivals, cost wise and product wise. It would now become the workshop of the world.

Clearly, what was needed was a theory of trade that was not only "politically correct," but one that was consistent with production theory as it stood after World War II. Finding his inspiration in Eli Heckscher and Bertil Ohlin's writings on endowments, Paul Samuelson outlined a new theory of trade, one based on endowments, and, more importantly, consistent with neo-classical production theory. Abstracting from the Ricardian reality of a technological asymmetries (i.e. a significantly more productive U.S. economy), and from non-negligible factor flows across countries, especially with the advent of the U.S. multinational corporation, Samuelson tied trade flows to immobile factor endowments. In a world of symmetric technology, countries that were well-endowed with capital would export capital-intensive goods, while those that were well-endowed with labor would export labor-intensive goods.

Whether by design or by accident, the model provided a water-tight rationale for U.S. dominance in manufacturing, namely its endowment of capital. Being more well-endowed than its trading partners, the U.S. would export manufactures, and import raw materials, which were presumedly more intensive in labor. Trade flows would be determined by factor endowments. Technology, the mainstay of Ricardo's work, was, as such, flushed from the debate.

What Samuelson had failed to realize, being essentially a theoretician, were several key developments in the resources sector. Specifically, raw material production processes had, with the advent of the electric motor and the internal combustion engine, become highly capital intensive, more so than manufacturing. Massive machinery and equipment, operated by relatively few employees, was used to extract and process raw materials, making for an extremely high capital/labor ratio. Relatively speaking, manufacturing was less capital intensive than raw materials.

Combined with the presence of important capital outflows, in the form of direct (foreign direct investment) and indirect (portfolio) investment, this had the perverse effect of making the United States a net importer of capital, and a net exporter of labor (i.e. the Leontief paradox). While this result is paradoxical within the context of the Heckscher-Ohlin-Samuelson model of trade, it is perfectly consistent with the predictions of the theory of vertical trade, as presented in Chapter 4.

7.3 Politics and Trade Theory

These findings raise a number of what I believe to be fundamental questions regarding trade theory. For example, if international trade has been and continues to be largely vertical in nature (resources for transformation), then why is this ignored in trade theory, whose purpose, after all, is to understand trade? Ricardian trade theory, Heckscher-Ohlin-Samuelson trade theory, and strategic trade theory continue to focus on trade in finished goods. Intermediate goods continue to be ignored.

There are, in my view, a number of factors, not the least of which is the overtly political nature of trade theory, beginning with David Ricardo's work in the early 1800's. Ricardian trade theory was not about science; instead, it was about what I choose to call trade network disequilibrium. As pointed out, the British trade network, at the beginning of the 19th century, no longer responded to the country's needs. While sugar, spices, rum, wood and furs still found the favor of the well-to-do, population growth in the late 18th century, combined with the rise of cotton as the preferred feedstock of the U.K. textile industry, rendered the existing trade network obsolete. Add to this the fact that colonies had proven costly for 18th century imperial powers (Britain and France). In short, what was needed was cheap (abundant) food and cheap (abundant) cotton, neither of which was available in the commonwealth.

The problem, however, was finding it, especially in light of the fact that (1) most of the world had, by then, been colonized, and (2) mercantile wars (i.e. between mercantile powers) were becoming costlier, the War of 1812 being a case in point.

Clearly, recolonizing the United States, a potential source of both food and cotton, was out of the question, politically and militarily. This led to the second-best (perhaps even first best) solution, namely abandoning the notion of geopolitical empire in favor of free-trade. This, in essence, was the purpose of classical trade theory: prove the optimality of free-trade over geopolitical network trade.

If successful, then the U.K. would have access to the abundant food and cotton of the United States, and other countries. Moreover, its comparative advantage in manufactures (terms of trade) would snuff out nascent industries in the United States and on the continent. If it failed, then, it would have no choice but to redefine (reconfigure) its empire.

As can be easily appreciated, a model of international trade in which resources are exchanged against value added (industrial trade) would have not found the favor of resource-exporting countries. Free-trade would have committed the latter to a future of subservience, and an uncertain future, given the historical volatility of resource markets.

The same is true of Heckscher-Ohlin-Samuelson trade theory, which, like Ricardian trade theory, ignores the industrial nature of world trade. Again, political factors are to blame.

As pointed out earlier, the United States emerged from World War II as the dominant industrial power. Its industry had flexed its muscles, muscles that had been atrophied by the Great Depression. Never before had the world seen as mighty an industrial giant. Unfortunately, there was a downside. For one, its internal supply of critical raw materials (e.g. iron ore) had dwindled. Second, new markets would be needed to vent its products.

Coincidentally, at roughly the same time, interest in trade was rising at MIT where Paul Samuelson was busy reworking the ideas of two Scandinavian economists (Eli Heckscher and Bertil Ohlin) into an analytical trade model. The result was the neoclassical trade model, known as the Heckscher-Ohlin trade model. Based on neoclassical production theory, comparative advantage was modeled in terms of factor endowments (capital and labor). The United States was seen as a capital-abundant country, while its trading partners were seen as labor abundant. Consequently, the United States would export capital-intensive goods and import labor-intensive goods. As in the Ricardian model, trade was Pareto improving.

The Heckscher-Ohlin model has since become the standard in trade theory, much like the Ricardian model had been prior to 1960. The problem, as pointed out earlier, is that it has been rejected, time and time again, by the data. Regardless of the data, regardless of the year, regardless of the countries, the model fails to explain trade patterns. Yet, in spite of this, it remains the cornerstone of modern trade theory (Markusen 1986).

This raises a number of questions, namely why? Why has it remained at the core of international trade theory despite the overwhelming evidence against it? The answer, I maintain, is partly related to politics, and partly related to science itself. Starting with the latter, science, like nature, abhors a vacuum. A bad theory is better than no theory at all. Combined with data problems, this has made for a situation in which the much-maligned Heckscher-Ohlin model remains, despite the overwhelming evidence against it, firmly entrenched at the center of trade theory. Returning to the former, namely politics, it must be remembered that despite its poor track record, the predictions of the Heckscher-Ohlin trade model are biased in favor of trade (i.e. are pro-trade), as were those of Ricardian trade analysis. A protectionist nation for most of its history, the U.S. embraced free-trade after World War II. Paul Samuelson, finding inspiration in the writings of mercantilist scholar Eli Heckscher and his student Bertil Ohlin, responded with a new justification for trade, namely endowment-based comparative advantage. Technology was irrelevant, or so Samuelson thought (Leamer, Bowen and Sveikauskas 1987; Telfer 1995). Trade, it therefore follows, was the result of exogenously-determined asymmetric endowments. In other words, to trade was natural.

It therefore follows that trade theory in general has little to do with trade and everything to do with trade policy. Industrial behemoths (U.K. and U.S.A.) have used gains from trade arguments to force trade on resource and energy-rich countries, hoping to maintain their advantage. Were they cut off from raw materials and energy, material wealth would literally dry up. Capital, as most physicists know, and management (upper-level and lower-level), are not physically productive.

7.4 Trade Theory as Ideology

Today, perhaps the greatest threat to the continued hegemony of the industrial nations (Group of six) is the specter of third-world industrialization. Were the resource and energy-producing nations of the world to transform their raw materials themselves, then the first world would be cut off and cut out. Having exhausted most of its commercially-feasible mineral and energy deposits, its standard of living would drop substantially. Take, for example, the case of Bauxite, the main raw material for aluminum. Neither of the G-6 countries has commercially-viable supplies, making them dependent on foreign supplies (Brazil, Australia, Jamaica, and Guinea).

One could argue that the ideology of free-trade is, in many regards, a intellectual hedge against such an eventuality, analogous to the "colonial diktat" of yore. A typical "colonial contract" or "colonial diktat" (see Bairoch (1997)) precluded autochthonous industrial development of the conquered parts of the world. According to Bairoch, the "colonial contract" was the main cause of non-transmission of industrial revolution outside Europe since it implied that (*a*) colonies could import only products from the metropolis and tariff rates had to be low, normally 0%, (*b*) colonial exports could be made only to the metropolis from which they could re-exported (*c*) production of manufacture goods that could compete with products of the metropolis was banned, and (*d*) transport between colony and metropolis was conducted only on metropolis ships. Economic policy of the colonies (to the extent that there was any independent economic policy) was therefore entirely subjugated to the interests of the metropolis, the most important objective being to prevent industrial competition from the colony.

Japan is a case in point. Were it to be cut off from imported raw materials and energy, its organization (capital, labor, and management) would be worthless—not to mention, useless. The G-6's wealth is increasingly dependent on imported raw materials and energy. Free trade, it therefore follows, makes perfect sense. By convincing third-world countries of the "Pareto optimality" of free trade, the West maintains, at least for a number of decades, its lease on life.

7.5 Consequences

Post-World War II developments, notably the GATT, the decolonization of Africa, the end of Keynesian economics and the rise of the multinational firm as the basic unit of international trade, have, as I argued earlier, ushered in a new era in international relations, one characterized by shallower geopolitical integration and deeper economic integration, the latter being the a result of the increasing presence of multinational firms. National borders, as Helliwell and others have seen, matter increasingly less. Firm borders, on the other hand, matter increasingly more, as evidenced by deeper vertical integration within firms (Multinational Firms).

These developments, seen as salutary by many, raise a number of theoretical questions, not the least of which is the question of viability, specifically, whether these developments are viable in the long run? Can centuries-old geopolitical networks be costlessly replaced by overlapping—geographically—economic networks (MNE's), and welfare increase? Is the past no longer relevant? Is history more or less bunk, as Henry Ford remarked?

To answer these and other questions, let me turn to the model of network institutions presented in Chapter 5. There, it was argued that there are no absolutes as far as network institutions go. In certain circumstances, deep integration is optimal, while in others, shallow integration is. The relevant question, as far as trade theory is concerned, is whether the current conditions warrant deep or shallow geopolitical institutions? Should governments progressively vacate the economic sphere in favor of MNE's, all the while removing all barriers to trade in stocks and flows, or should they maintain some form of control?

As pointed out in Chapter 3, deep institutions are warranted in the presence of public goods and coordination failures. As was the case in ancient Sumeria and ancient Rome, the presence of public goods resulted in deep network institutions in the form of geopolitical-economic empires. In the 20th century, the Great Depression, and the birth of the modern welfare state contributed to further deepening the social network. World War II did likewise.

The question is whether today such conditions are present, or are wont to be? Clearly, the push for less government in most western industrialized nations, nullifies the first condition, namely, the free-rider problem. With fewer public goods, the need for deeper (or deep) network institutions is less. Included in public goods is what I choose to refer to as equity, that is, economic equity (income redistribution). The brings us to the question of coordination failures. Specifically, are there coordination failures looming on the horizon? As I pointed out in Chapter 3, the presence of coordination failures militates in favor of deeper geopolitical institutions. Can multinational firms with minimal government intervention successfully conduct the affairs of the world economy, ensuring continued growth, full employment, and a reasonable distribution of wealth, not to mention, meet minimum health and safety criteria?

To most observers, the answer to this question is an unqualified yes. Governments around the world have, over the past decade, adopted pro-business agendas, and, in many cases, have become partners, leaving in the wake, the confrontational attitudes of the post-World War II period. Anti-trust policy has, for all intents and purposes, been abandoned, as have other forms of regulation. Governments, far from discouraging mergers, encourage them, arguing that what is good for business is ultimately good for society as a whole.

There are, however, glitches, some of which are more notable than others. For example, there is the Asian crisis, which observers agree put an end to the Asian miracle. Currencies in the Asian tigers collapsed, as did the stock markets. The euphoria subsided. Today, the Japanese economy is mired in recession, as are a number of Asian dragons. Clearly, something went wrong.

How did the world react? Paradoxically, by deepening institutional ties, specifically, by creating the Group of 20, the purpose of which was to enlarge the breadth of the Group of 7 countries. The upshot was relatively simple, namely that the North (i.e. industrialized countries) could no longer ignore the South when it came time to policy. More to the point, the North and the South would have to coordinate, jointly, fiscal and monetary policy.

Another glitch is the recent energy crisis, and, more specifically, the U.S. policy reaction. While the Bush administration is decidedly pro-free market, it nonetheless has decided that in the name of national security and welfare, a continental energy policy, which would include its neighbors, Canada and Mexico, is warranted, this providing an example of welfare-increasing deep integration and, as such, deep institutions.

While these crises have done little to alter, in any significant way, the generally-accepted view of the role of markets in the creation of wealth, they have nonetheless introduced doubt. Doubt over the ability of private agents (firms) to govern themselves in the absence of institutions.

Add to this the explosion of regional trade agreements (Mercosur, European Union, FTAA, APEC), and what you get is a sense that institutions are important, specifically, that institutions go to the heart of who and what we are as a species.

7.6 Free Trade as an Instrument of Network Realignment

If geopolitical networks play, as argued in this book, an important role in trade, then this raises an important question, namely how should one understand the current free-trade rhetoric? Why do countries that espouse free trade, enact measures which, in many regards, serve to limit trade? The reason, I contend, has to do with what I refer to as network realignment. To understand why, suppose that to begin with, the world is carved out in terms of geopolitical-economic networks, networks that are independent of each other. Also suppose that for some reason, one of the empires undergoes a technology shock that is such that it now requires more feed-stocks of energy and raw materials. The choices open to it are limited, and include, military invasion, political diplomacy, or, lastly, ideological warfare. The least costly is, of course, the latter. Freedom, considered a universal virtue, has, since the mid-19th century, been the most favored ideology.

A good example of this is Africa with its abundant energy and raw materials. Prior to World War II, most of the African continent had been carved up among European industrial networks, with Britain and France being the most prominent.[3] The United States was, for all intents and purposes, excluded. While this was not perceived of to be a problem at the time, things would evolve in such a way as to make it one. U.S. economic growth in the 20th century increased the demand for industrial feedstocks, and, in the process, spurred U.S. interests in Africa. The problem, however, was one of access. Africa was part of European networks. To get around this, it, much like the British in the 19th century, advocated democracy and free trade. Democracy would rid the countries of colonial rule, and free trade would open markets that had been hitherto closed. Theoretically, at least, these measures were intended to liberate the peoples of Africa of their former oppressors, and provide them with political and economic choice. The problem, however, is that energy and raw material markets characterized by a large number of buyers and sellers do not exist. As Carmine Nappi and Marian Radeski have pointed out, raw materials are rarely traded in the open market, but, instead, are traded within firms. Once freed of their former colonial oppressors, African nations had little choice but to deal with the United States.

The point here is relatively simple, namely that free trade has been, and continues to be, a form of network realignment, one couched in ideals, and less costly for industrialized countries than the alternative instruments of military invasion or political diplomacy.

7.6.1 Geopolitical Networks and Efficiency

Once could go as far as to argue that globalization, defined as the joint occurrence of multinational firms and minimum geopolitical networks, is optimal in the sense of network realignment, defined earlier. Specifically, define latter-day empires as consisting of the set of multinational firms with headquarters in a geo-political network. Also, assume that MNE's and governments cooperate in creating wealth. That is, governments adopt policies that are favorable to their multinational firms.

The result is a world of overlapping economic networks. U.S. MNE's are present in Europe, and European MNE's are present in the United States. Trade need no longer be conducted in well-defined geo-political networks, as had been the case since the beginning of civilization.

Network realignment is in these circumstances apolitical. The market would be the ultimate arbitrator, channeling resources to the highest bidder.

7.7 Implications for International Finance

The implications of Chapters 1–6 for international finance, or the financing of trade, are extensive, including the very basis on which the theory of international finance is erected, namely spontaneous large-scale exchange among sovereign nations. As I have attempted to demonstrate, historically, theoretically, and empirically, large-scale international exchange has never been conducted in a Walrasian market setting. Put differently, international trade has, for the most part, never been spontaneous in nature, but, rather, has been conducted within geopolitical, economic, or geopolitical-economic (multinationals) networks. The crucial feature, as far as international finance is concerned, is the fact that exchange within the relevant network has, for the most part, been carried out in the currency of the relevant *manufacturia*, the implication being that *primerias'* currencies have been largely irrelevant. In many cases, primerias' did not have currencies of their own, and, as such, used the relevant network currency (British Pound, French Franc). In cases involving inter-network ownership (i.e. 19th century British trading companies, multinational firms), exchange has been amonetary (not involved money), consisting of no more than an accounting entry. In other words, little to no money was actually exchanged. As multinational firms today oversee seventy percent of world trade, it stands to reason that trade flows are, by the very nature of exchange, irrelevant to the value of a nation's currency.

This, I believe, explains the profession's inability to understand exchange rate behavior in Mundell-Felming terms (Messe and Rogoff 1983). While the values of trade and factor flows are, in fact, reported in domestic currencies, the bulk of the actual trading is either non-financial (i.e. involves bookkeeping), or involves an international currency, such as the U.S. dollar, the German mark, or the Japanese yen. It is conceivable that a large U.S. multinational firm could double its shipments to the U.S. from its Canadian subsidiary without increasing its demand for Canadian dollars.[4]

The point I wish to make here is simple, namely that trade flows do not occur between agents (firms) of sovereign countries in what are Walrasian markets, but, rather, occur within well-defined networks (multinationals). As such, models of international currency markets based on such premises are bound to come up short. That the profession has failed to model exchange rates, as such, comes as no surprise. In fact, what would be surprising is that any of these models would even work, given their questionable theoretical underpinnings.

The implications are straightforward, namely that currency markets should be seen as extensions of asset markets. Currency values, as such, are more apt to vary in response to arbitrage conditions than in response to trade flows.

7.8 Conclusions

The joint presence of multinational firms, regional trading agreements, and multilateral geopolitical-economic organizations (United Nations, WTO, OECD) are, I argue, testimonies to the integral role of networks in trade, corroborating thousands of years of history and evolution. We as a species are traders, and the basis of our trading activity is the neural network, where information is stored, processed, and retrieved. This leads me to the rather strong conclusion that networks and trade are indissoluble. Removing networks from trade would be the equivalent of removing the neo-cortex from our brain, with similar results, namely the end of trading (social) activity.

8

Summary and Conclusions

For over 300,000 years, we as a species have traded in well-defined and well-structured networks. For over 35,000 years, network trade has, for the most part, been dictated by the exigencies of industry, with up-stream natural resources being traded against down-stream transformation, more commonly known as value added. For over 6,000 years, network trade has been conducted in well-defined geopolitical entities, whether they be city-states, empires, countries, etcetera, and have been mediated by fiat money. For the last 150 years, attempts have been made to alter the nature of such trade, particularly with regard to the role played by government, all the while preserving the nature of the underlying trade, namely being carried out in well-defined networks, the multinational firm being the most common form.

Paradoxically, the study of trade has, for all intents and purposes, been devoid of networks. From very early on, trade was modelled as a spontaneous activity, having little to do with government (networks). In fact, with the passage of time, government became synonymous with inertia and Pareto-inferior equilibria.

In this book, I have attempted, using historical, theoretical, and empirical methods, to recast the theory of international trade in terms of network theory, and, in the process, shed light on the puzzles which have now become common-place in economics in general, and international economics in particular. The upshot is relatively simple, namely that networks have mattered, do matter, and, undoubtedly, will continue to matter in the future. Networks define who we are as a species, distinguishing us from our simian cousins, and now-extinct forbearers. Society, as we know it, is itself a trade network, made possible by the unique trade-accounting device which is the human neo-cortex. That the trading networks that we as a species devised and continue to devise should be analogous to our social networks, should not, as such, come as a surprise. The historical record is clear: the ascent of man has been increasing in the size of the relevant network.

The larger the network, the greater the achievements, as evidenced by Sumer, Egypt, Rome, the United States, etcetera.

Evidence of the role of networks in contemporary world trade has, as pointed out in Chapter 4, been provided, albeit indirectly, from the "border effects" literature. As has been shown, networks matter; more to the point, networks matter more than is commonly believed.

Trade theory, it is felt, cannot be at odds with the findings of neuropsychology, evolutionary psychology, anthropology, and ancient and modern history, for obvious reasons, not the least of which is consistency. For if the way we trade in commodities is fundamentally different from the way we trade in, say, social settings, then somewhere, sometime, something changed. And, until someone, somewhere can show that indeed, there was a shift, then unity and consilience of science must be invoked.

The findings presented in this book, especially the theorems in Chapter 3, and the model presented in Chapter 4, will appear, to some, to be iconoclastic, contrasting, and, indeed, contradicting accepted wisdom. I, however, beg to disagree. In fact, I would argue that if there ever was a body of iconoclastic thought in trade theory, it was associated with the names of Adam Smith, David Ricardo, Eli Heckscher and Bertil Ohlin, to name a few. Theoretically speaking, trade cannot be free, free of government, owing to, among other things, the ubiquitous coordination failures that characterize social activity. Coordination failure-resolving governments, far from hindering the progress of civilization, are, in my view, at the very root of civilization.

That trade theory has, for the most part, been less than successful owes, in no small part, to the inability on the part of the above writers to first acknowledge, and, second, appreciate the historical record. To argue, without so much as a shred of evidence, that free markets Pareto-dominate mercantilism and indeed, all other forms of social and economic organization, was and continues to be, in my view, erroneous not to mention non-scientific.

I begin by summarizing my principal findings. This is then followed by a number of conclusions.

1.   Homo sapiens-sapiens is, by nature, a social being, trading in well-defined networks. Further, the neocortex (neo-pallium) is, in large measure, a trade-related neurological organ.

2.   The optimal size of trade networks is determined, in large measure, by a species' ability to transmit, store and retrieve information. The greater is the latter, the greater is the resulting trade network. This provides a neuro-

logical basis for Adam Smith's belief in an inate propensity to truck, barter and trade.

3.   The invention of writing greatly increased the optimal size of networks, paving the way for large-scale specialization and exchange.

4.   Markets as we know them today do not arise spontaneously as is commonly thought.

5.   Governments, being the architects of markets, seek to control trade, both internal and external.

6.   Governments create trade networks, and encourage internal-to-network trade, and discourage external-to-network trade. With the creation of transnational companies, this was no longer the case, as governments were able to tax foreign earnings.

7.   The historical record is replete with examples of network trade creation. U.S. strategic interests are a case in point.

8.   Implications for trade theory: abandon the notion of a single, global Walrasian market, in which comparative advantage is the principal arbitrator, in favor of trade networks in which trade flows are determined by the relative price of value added (*manufacturia*) to raw materials (*primaria*). As factors (energy, capital, and labor) are mobile within the trade network, their geographic abundance has no bearing on the direction of trade.

9.   Idea of overlapping networks (Chinese 19th century concessions). Trade networks are increasingly economic in nature, having been divorced from geopolitical networks via free-trade. As such, trade networks and geopolitical networks are no longer concentric.

10. Weakening of the geopolitical aspects of trade networks. Trade networks are no longer, forcibly, political networks-institutions.

11. Multinationals, however, will be the 21st century equivalents of the great geopolitical trading empires.

To conclude, heightened trade activity is as old as our species; in fact, it is what defines our species. While the bottle of trade had evolved over time, in response to various stimuli, the wine has remained the same. World trade patterns today differ little from those of ancient times. Networks mattered then, matter now, and undoubtedly, will continue to matter.

Endnotes

Chapter 1

1. This is consistent with Granovetter's view that all economic action is embedded in networks. See Granovetter (1985).

2. By large-scale organized trade, it should be understood trade that takes place in the presence of well-defined trading institutions such as the presence of specialized merchants. Such trade stands in stark contrast with spontaneous trade carried out without such institutions. An example of the latter is spontaneous trade among neighboring farmers, exchanging say eggs for butter.

3. The result is a game-theoretical rationale for Karl Polanyi's notion of "embeddedness." Specifically, markets are not spontaneous in nature, but, instead, result from government via public goods. See Polanyi (1944).

Chapter 2

1. One could define network in institutional terms. According to John R. Commons:

   > If we endeavor to find a universal circumstance, common to all behavior known as institutional, we may define an institution as collective action in control, liberation and expansion of individual action. Collective action ranges all the way from unorganized custom to the many organized going concerns, such as the family, the corporation, the trade association, the trade union, the reserve system, the state. The principle common to all of them is greater or less control, liberation and expansion of individual action by collective action.

   The public good in this case would be the structure of the trading environment itself.

2. Another way of looking at these activities is in terms of basic mechanics. In each case, networking confers a force-related advantage on the group.

Combining the physical force of two or more individuals increases the set of feasible activities (physical).

3. For more on the question of annexation or conquest, see Grossman and Mendoza (2001).

4. One should this period as one of competitive religions and of competitive gods.

5. Interestingly, in 1786, representatives from five newly-formed states met at Annapolis, Maryland, to discuss interstate trade. Because so few representatives attend, Alexander Hamilton and James Madison called for another convention to be held in Philadelphia. In 1787, the Constitutional Convention begins on May 25, in Philadelphia. Fifty-five representatives attend and begin drafting the Constitution. On September 17, 1787, the convention comes to a close as the representatives sign the Constitution.

6. The St-Maurice river valley in Quebec (Shawinigan) owed its development in the early part of the 20 century to U.S. foreign direct investment, notably by the Duke family, owners of American Tobacco.

Chapter 3

1. It is interesting to note that the work autarky and autism have the same Greek root, namely autos, meaning self. Put differently, autism, like autarky, is characterized by the absence of exchange.

2. As pointed out in Chapter 1, Homo sapiens sapiens are, by definition, capable of social behavior. That is, they have large neo-cortexes, and, secondly, can write and keep records. This rules out the trade impossibility theorem presented earlier.

3. These are commonly referred to as "I'll go if you go" strategies (Suk-Young Chwe 2000).

4. One could argue that the sex-based marketing which has become ubiquitous in our society, free rides on the gains from gender-based trade.

5. Implicitly, it is assumed that the primary market involves the government as buyer or seller.

6. Outstanding merchant credit is, by design, equal to national income.

7. This result, I argue, underlies the 19th and 20th century interest in institutional economics. For example, Thornstein Veblen's interest in institutional economics, specifically in the institutions of capitalism, resulted from the perceived of inability of capitalism to move the U.S. economy on to the new, higher equilibrium growth path defined by the electrification of U.S. industry. Such was also the cause of Robert Owen's interest in reforming social institutions.

8. As pointed out earlier, the size of tribes and bands was (is) determined in large part by the human brain's capacity to store and retrieve member-specific information.

9. This view is consistent with the basic tenets of institutional economics. According to John R. Commons:

> Stated in the language of ethics and law, to he developed below, all collective acts establish relations of rights, duties, no rights and no duties. Stated in the language of individual behavior, what they require is performance, avoidance, forbearance by individuals. Stated in the language of the resulting economic status of individuals, what they provide is security, conformity, liberty and exposure. Stated in language of cause, effect or purpose, the common principles running through all of them are the principles of scarcity, efficiency, futurity, the working rules of collective action and the limiting and complementary factors of economic theory. Stated in language of the operation of working rules on individual action, they are expressed by the auxiliary verbs of what the individual can, cannot, must, do. cannot," because collective action will or will not come to his aid. He "must" or "must not," because collective action will compel him. He "may," because collective action will permit him and protect him. He "may not," because collective action will prevent him. Put differently, collective choice is synonymous with civilization.

10. The transition from taxation in kind to taxation in the form of legal tender, is examined in detail in a forthcoming book entitled *Trade and Civilization, The Origins of Government, Markets and Money.*

11. This view of the emergence of money differs markedly from that found in the literature (Howitt and Clower 2000)

12. Temples and temple activities provided a centralized local for trade activity. Wor shipers would bring goods as their offering to the priests and would trade surpluses.

13. A good example of this is classical political economy which was, in essence, a reaction to mercantilism. Classical economists railed against government, never once stopping to consider the very raison d'être of government. Perhaps once, mercantilism had been optimal. Perhaps once, it had been a dominant strategy.

14. This is true of the lower primates, other mammals, and other life forms (i.e. reptiles).

15. Like Joseph Schumpeter, I am unreserved in my praise for John Law. The ideas developed in *Money and Trade Considered*, I maintain, run parallel to those developed in this chapter, namely that money and large-scale exchange are synonymous.

16. One could argue that the tariff, being a tax, was originally levied as an attempt to recover lost tax revenue from extra-network trade.

17. For more on this (plunder or negotiation), see Herschel I. Grossman and Juan Mendoza's NBER paper, *Annexation or Conquest? The Economics of Empire Building.*"

Chapter 4

1. This is referred to as vertical trade as opposed to horizontal trade (i.e. trade in finished goods).

2. The choice of a Leontief technology here was motivated, in large measure, by its aggregative properties (i.e. Leontief aggregation.

3. Constrast this with the production technology found in Hummels, Rapoport and Yi (1998), Hummels, Ishii and Yi (2001), where labor is the only variable factor input.

4. The relative price of value added in the manufacturing region, the relative price of value added in the intermediate product region and the relative price of the raw material, expressed in terms of the final product (i.e. $y(t)$), are as follows, respectively:

$$\frac{P_v}{\delta P_v + \gamma\lambda[R(0),R(t)]P_{v_m} + \gamma\mu P_v}$$

$$\frac{P_{v_m}}{\delta P_v + \gamma\lambda[R(0),R(t)]P_{v_m} + \gamma\mu P_v}$$

$$\frac{P_r}{\delta P_v + \gamma\lambda[R(0),R(t)]P_{v_m} + \gamma\mu P_v}$$

5. See for example Beaudreau (1998).

6. As Kei-Mu Yi (2003) has pointed out, the spectacular growth in world trade in the 1990's was driven in large measure by vertical as opposed to horizontal trade.)

7. Another way of seeing distribution is as the final (ultimate) level of value added that is, before the consumer receives the product. The better any given manufacuria is at distribution, the greater is its comparative advantage.

8. One could go one step further and attribute the latter (process and product technology) to knowledge in general, and managerial knowledge in particular. As I pointed out in earlier work (Beaudreau 1989), countries that are well-endowed with innovative managers—as opposed to routine managers—are more likely to be downstream value adders, and vice-versa. Moreover, the more a country has of such managers, the more likely is it to enjoy a comparative advantage vis-a-vis other *manufacturias*.

9. It is worthwhile noting that such a case, described in detail by British political economists in the 19th century, is the exception, and not the rule in so far as international vertical trade. The historical record seems to show that vertical trade has, since time immemorial, been carried out in well-defined networks, be they empires or integrated, multinational firms.

10. See Rauch and Casella (2003), Rauch and Trindale (2002), and Weidenbaum and Hughes (1996).

Chapter 5

1.   Distribution is, as such, to be viewed as a downstream value-adding transformation activity.

2.   One could go one step further and attribute the latter (process and product technology) to knowledge in general, and managerial knowledge in particular. As I pointed out in earlier work (Beaudreau 1989), countries that are well-endowed with innovative managers—as opposed to routine managers—are more likely to be downstream value adders, and vice-versa.

3.   Following in the footsteps of Bertil Ohlin, we view regional and international trade to be analytically equivalent.

4.   Clearly, this is a second-best solution as some states may transform raw materials, as well as produce manufactured goods.

5.   These measures are simply weighted averages of the electric power-labor and capital-labor ratios, the weights being the share of industry exports/imports in total ex-ports/imports by country.

6.   The remaining 3.6 percent is accounted for by stock draw-down.

7.   One could argue that the absence of intermediate goods in conventional trade models is partly responsible for this situation. After all, theoretical considerations, in large measure, determine data requirements.

Chapter 6

1.   One could argue that manufacturias assume the role of Stackelberg leader while primarias assume the role of Stackelberg followers.

2.   What is particularly ironic is the fact that the campaign to end slavery began in the North, in places like Boston and New York, and not in the South. Clearly, the underlying motives were economic, having little to do with human rights.

3.   As I argue in Beaudreau (1999), the electrification of the United States at the turn of the century led to increased interstate trade, which, in turn, prompted a number of important institutional changes (tools of trade),

including the Federal Reserve Act of 1913, which established a single national currency.

4. In fact, one could argue that its foreign policy leading up to World War II was an example of industrial network building.

5. As a result, it ran balance of payments surpluses with the United States, and balance of payment deficits with resource-supplying countries.

6. Proof of this view is comes by way of the very origins of the anti-slavery movement, which, oddly enough, began in Boston.

Chapter 7

1. One could go as far as labelling it propaganda, not having any basis in science. It is interesting to note that the free-trade movement in Great Britain in the 1830's began as a merchant-sponsored anti-corn law society, the purpose of which was to rid England of the infamous corn laws that had contributed to raising the cost of living and, consequently, real wages.

2. See Innis (1930, 1940)

3. An multilateral agreement on borders was reached at the Berlin Conference in 1884. These borders are those that exist today.

4. For example, it could simply raise the necessary trade credit in Canada.

Bibliography

Adelson, Howard. 1962. *Medieval Commerce*. Princeton, NJ: Van Nostrand.

Aghion, Philippe. and Peter Howitt. 1998. *Endogenous Growth Theory*. Cambridge, MA: MIT Press.

Aiello, Leslie C. and Peter Wheeler. 1995. The Expensive-tissue hypothesis. *Current Anthropology* 36:199–221.

Aiello, Leslie C. and Robin I. M. Dunbar. 1993. Neocortex Size, Group Size and the Evolution of Language in Hominids. *Current Anthropology* 34:101–104.

Akerlof, George & Rachel Kranton. 2000. Economics and identity. *Quarterly Journal of Economics* 115:715-753.

Armstrong, D.M. 1981. *Belief, Truth and Knowledge*. Cambridge: Cambridge University Press.

Aumann, R. and R. Myerson. 1988. Endogenous formation of links between players and coalitions: An application of the Shapley Value," In: Roth, A. (Ed.) *The Shapley Value*. Cambridge: Cambridge University Press.

Bairoch, P. 1997. *Victoires and déhoires* (3 vols.). Paris: Gallimard.

Bala, V. and S. Goyal. 2000. A strategic analysis of network reliability. *Review of Economic Design* 5:205–228.

Bala, V. and S. Goyal. 2000. A non-cooperative model of network formation. *Econometrica* 68:1181-1231.

Balassa, B., and M. Noland. 1988. *Japan in the World Economy*. Washington, DC: Institute for International Economics.

Baron-Cohen, S. 1991. Precursors to a theory of mind: Understanding attention in others," in Whitten, A. (Ed.) *Natural Theories of Mind*. Oxford: Basil Blackwell.

Barkow, J.H., L. Cosmides and J. Tooby. 1998. (Eds.) *The Adapted Mind: Evolutionary Psychology and the Generation of Culture*. Oxford: Oxford University Press.

Barkow, J.H. 1984. The distance between genes and culture. *Journal of Anthropological Research* 37:367–379.

Beaudreau, Bernard C. 1989. Entrepreneurial ability, international trade, and foreign direct investment. *International Economic Journal* 3:1–22.

Beaudreau, Bernard C. 1995. The impact of electric power on productivity: The case of U.S. manufacturing 1958–1984. *Energy Economics* 17:231–236.

Beaudreau, Bernard C. 1996. *Mass Production, The Stock Market Crash, and The Great Depression: The Macroeconomics of Electrification*. Westport, CT: Greenwood Press.

Beaudreau, Bernard C. 1998. *Energy and Organization: Growth and Distribution Reexamined*. Westport, CT: Greenwood Press.

Beaudreau, Bernard C. 1999. *Energy and the Rise and Fall of Political Economy*. Westport, CT: Greenwood Press.

Beiser, Arthur. 1983. *Modern Technical Physics*. Menlo Park, California: The Benjamin/Cummings Publishing Company.

Berndt, Ernst and David O. Wood. 1975. Technology, prices and the derived demand for energy. *The Review of Economics and Statistics* 259–268.

Bonacich, Phillip. 1998. Four kinds of social dilemmas within exchange networks. *Current Research in Social Psychology* 1:1–7.

Bonacich, Phillip. 1998. The evolutionary stability of strategies in exchange networks. *Current Research in Social Psychology* 3:12–34.

Bowen, Harry P., Edward Leamer, and Leo Sveikauskas. 1987. Multicountry, multifactor tests of the factor abundance theory. *American Economic Review* 77:791–809.

Brecher, Richard A. and Choudri, Ehsan U. 1988. The factor content of consumption in Canada and the United States: A two-country test of the Heckscher-

Ohlin-Vanek model. in Robert C. Feenstra (Ed.) *Empirical Methods for International Trade*. Cambridge, MA: MIT Press.

Brentano, F. 1960. The distinction between mental and physical phenomena. in Chisholm, R.M., (Ed.), *Realism and Background in Phenomenology*. Glencoe, IL: Free Press.

Bryne, R., and A. Whiten, (Eds.) 1988. *Machiavellian Intelligence*. Oxford: Clarendon.

Buchanan, James M. 1965. An economic theory of clubs. *Economica* 1–18.

Calvin, William H. 1998. The emergence of intelligence. *Scientific American Presents* 9:44–51.

Casella, A. and Rauch, J. 2002. Anonymous market and group ties in international trade. *Journal of International Economics* 58:19-47.

Caves, Richard E. 1982. *Multinational Enterprise and Economic Analysis*. Cambridge, Cambridge University Press.

Chaliland, Grard et Jean-Pierre Rageau. 1993. *Atlas des Empires de la Baltique la Russie sovietique*. Paris: Payot.

Commons, John R. 1931. Institutional economics. *American Economic Review*l 21:648-657.

Cosmides, Leda and John Tooby, 1992, "Cognitive Adaptations for Social Exchange," pp. 163-228 in Barkow, Cosmides and Tooby, eds.

Cosmides, Leda and John Tooby. 1998. *Evolutionary Psychology: A Primer*, http://www.psych.ucsb.edu/research/cep/primer.html.

Davern, Michael. 1997. Social networks and economic sociology: a proposed research agenda for more complete social science. *The American Journal of Economics and Sociology*.

deDuve, Christian. 1995. The beginnings of life on earth. *American Scientist*, September-October.

Devine, Warren D. 1990. Electricity in information management: The evolution of electronic control,", in Schurr, Sam. H. et al. (eds.), *Electricity in the American Economy*. Westport CT: Greenwood Press.

Dudley, Leonard. 1991. *The Word and The Sword: How Techniques of Information and Violence Have Shaped our World*. Oxford: Basil Blackwell.

Dunbar, Robin. 1988. *Primate Social Systems*. London: Chapman Hall.

Dunbar, Robin. 1992. Neocortex size as a constraint on group size in primates. *Journal of Human Evolution* 22:469-493.

Dunbar, Robin. 1993. Co-evolution of neocortex size, group size and language in humans. *Behavioral and Brain Sciences* 681-735.

Duncan, Colin A. M., and David W. Tandy. 1994. *From Political Economy to Anthropology*. London: Black Rose Books.

Dunning, J.H. 1981. *International Production and the Multinational Enterprise*. London, George Allen and Unwin.

Ellison, G. 1993. Learning, local interaction, and coordination. *Econometrica* 61:1047-1071.

Facts on File, *Atlas of the British Empire*. New York.

Feldstein, M. and C. Horioka. 1980. Domestic saving and international capital flows. *Economic Journal* 90:314-29.

Findlay, Ronald. 1978. An Austrian model of international trade and interest rate equalization. *Journal of Political Economy* 86:989–1008.

Findlay, Ronald. 1984. Growth and development in trade models. in Jones, R.W. and P.B. Kenen. (Eds.) *Handbook of International Economics*. Elsevier Science Publishers.

Fischman, Leonard. 1980. *World Mineral Trends & U. S. Supply Problems*. Baltimore, MD: Johns Hopkins University Press.

Garnsey, Peter, Keith Hopkins, and C.R. Whittaker. 1983. *Trade in the Ancient Economy*. Berkeley, CA: University of California Press.

Garreau, Joel. 1981. *The Nine Nations of North America*. New York: Avon.

Gelb, I. J. 1963. *A Study of Writing*. Chicago, IL: University of Chicago Press.

Gigerenzer, Gerd and Klaus Hug. 1992. Domain-specific reasoning: Social contracts, cheating, and perspective change. *Cognition* 43:127–171.

Goffart, Walter. 1974. *Caput and Colonae, Towards a History of Late Roman Taxation*. Toronto: University of Toronto Press.

Gollop, F.M., and D. W. Jorgenson. 1980. U.S. productivity growth by industry, 1948–1973," in Kendrick, J.W., and Vaccara, B.N. (Eds.) *New Developments in Productivity Measurement and Analysis*. Chicago, IL: National Bureau of Economic Research.

Granovetter, Mark. 1985. Economic action and social structure. *American Journal of Sociology* 91:481–510.

Greenwood, Jeremy and Bruce D. Smith. 1997. Financial Markets in Development, and the Development of Financial Markets," *Journal of Economic Dynamics and Control*, 21, 1997, 145-181.

Grossman, Herschel and Juan Mendoza. 2001. Annexation or Conquest? The Economics of Empire Building, NBER Working Paper 8109, Cambridge, MA: NBER.

Gullickson, William and Michael J. Harper. 1988. Multifactor productivity in U.S. manufacturing, 1949–1983. *Monthly Labor Review* 18–28.

Harden, Donald. 1962. *The Phoenicians*. London: Thames and Hudson.

Harkness, Jon. 1982. The factor-proportions model with many nations, goods and factors: Theory and evidence. *Review of Economics and Statistics* 298–305.

Heckscher, Eli F. 1919. The effect of foreign trade on the distribution of income. *Ekonomisk Tidskrif* 21:1–32.

Helliwell, John F. 1998. *How Much Do National Borders Matter?* Washington, DC: Brookings Institution Press.

Helliwell, John F. 1999. National Borders, Trade and Migration, NBER Working Paper W6027.

Helliwell, John F. 2002. Border Effects: Assessing Their Implications for Canadian Policy in a North-American Context, manuscript, University of British Columbia.

Helpman, Elhanan. 1996. Politics and Trade Policy, NBER Working Paper 5309.

Helpman, Elhanan (Ed.). 1998. *General Purpose Technologies and Economic Growth*. Cambridge MA: MIT Press.

Helpman, Elhanan and Manuel Trajtenberg. 1994. A Time to Sow and a Time to Reap: Growth Based on General Purpose Technologies. *National Bureau of Economic Research Working Paper* No. 4854.

Helpman, Elhanan. 1999. The structure of foreign trade. *Journal of Economic Perspectives* 13:121–144.

Hounshell, David A. 1984. *From the American System to Mass Production 1800–1932: The Development of Manufacturing Technology in the United States*. Baltimore, MD: The Johns Hopkins University Press.

Howitt, Peter, and Robert Clower. 2000. The emergence of economic organization. *Journal of Economic Behavior and Organization* 41:55-84.

Hummels, David, Ishii, Jun, and Yi, Kei-Mu. 2001. The nature and growth of vertical specialization in world trade. *Journal of International Economics* 54:75–96.

Hummels, David, Rapoport, Dana, and Yi, Kei-Mu. 1998. Vertical specialization and the changing nature of world trade. *Federal Reserve Bank of New York Economic Policy Review* 4:79-99.

Innis, Harold A. 1930. *The Fur Trade in Canada: An Introduction to Canadian Economic History*. New Haven, CT: Yale University Press.

Innis, Harold A. 1940. *The Cod Fisheries: The History of an International Economy*. New Haven, CT: Yale University Press.

International Institute for Environment and Development, Producing and Selling Minerals, MMSD Draft, March 4, 2002.

Jackson, Matthew O. 2003. A Survey of Models of Network Formation: Stability and Efficiency. In Gabrielle Demange and Myrna Wooders. (Eds.) *Group Formation in Economics: Networks, Clubs, and Coalitions.* Cambridge: Cambridge University Press.

Jorgenson, Dale W. 1983. Energy prices and productivity growth," in Schurr, S. et al. (Eds.) *Energy, Productivity, and Economic Growth.* Cambridge, MA: Oelgeschlager, Gunn, and Hain.

Jorgenson, D.W. 1981.The Role of Energy in Productivity Growth. in Kendrick, J.W. (Ed.) *International Comparisons of Productivity and Causes of the Slowdown.* Cambridge MA: MIT Press.

Kali, Raja. 1999. Endogenous business networks. *Journal of Law, Economics and Organization* 15: 615–36.

Kemp, Murray C. 1984. The Role of Natural Resources in Trade Models. in Jones, R.W. and P.B. Kenen. (Eds.) *Handbook of International Economics.* Elsevier Science Publishers.

Kenwood, A.G. et A.L. Lougheed. 1992. *The Growth of the International Economy 1820–1990.* London: Routledge.

Klein, Philip A. & Geoffrey H. Moore. 1985. *Monitoring Growth Cycles in Market-Oriented Countries: Developing and Using International Economic Indicators.* Cambridge, MA: Ballinger Publishing Co.

Kranton, Rachel. 1996. Reciprocal Exchange: A Self-Sustaining System. *American Economic Review* 86:130-851.

Kranton, Rachel E., and Deborah F. Minehart. 2000. A theory of buyer-seller networks." *American Economic Review.*

Krugman, Paul. 1980. Scale economies, product differentiation, and the pattern of trade. *American Economic Review* 70:950–959.

Krugman, Paul. 1981. Trade, accumulation and uneven development. *Journal of Development Economics* 149–161.

Lagunoff, Roger. 2000. On the evolution of Pareto-optimal behavior in repeated coordination problems. *International Economic Review* 11:273–293.

Landes, David S. 1980. The great drain and industrialization: Commodity flows from periphery to center in historical perspective," in R.C.O. Matthews (Ed.) *Economic Growth and Resources, Trends and Factors*. London: MacMillan.

Law, John. 1705. *Money and Trade Considered with a Proposal for Supplying the Nation with Money*. Edinburgh: Heirs and Successors of Andrew Anderson.

Lawrence, R.Z. 1987. Imports in Japan: Closed markets or closed minds. *Brookings Papers on Economic Activity* 517–558.

Leamer, Edward E. 1980. The Leontief paradox reconsidered. *Journal of Political Economy* 88:495–503.

Leamer, Edward E. 1984. *Sources of International Comparative Advantage: Theory and Evidence*. Cambridge: MIT Press.

Leamer, Edward E. and Harry P. Bowen. 1981. Cross-section tests of the Heckscher-Ohlin theorem: Comment. *American Economic Review* 71:1040–1043.

Lennie, Peter. 2003. The cost of cortical computation. *Current Biology* 13:493–497.

Leontief, Wassily W. 1953. Domestic production and foreign trade: The American capital position reexamined. *Proceedings of the American Philosophical Society* 97:332–349.

List, George Friedrich. 1856. *National System of Political Economy*. Philadelphia, PA: Lippincott.

Maddison, Angus. 1987. Growth and slowdown in advanced capitalist economies: Techniques of quantitative assessment. *Journal of Economic Literature* 25:649–698.

MacLean, Paul. 1990. *The Triune Brain in Evolution*. New York: Plenum Press.

Markusen, James R. 1986. Explaining the volume of trade: An eclectic approach. *American Economic Review* 76:1002–1032.

McCallum, John. 1995. National borders matter: Canada-U.S. regional trade patterns. *American Economic Review* 85:615–623.

Meijer Fik et Onno van Nijf. 1992. *Trade, Transport and Society in the Ancient World, A Sourcebook*. London: Routledge.

Messe, R. A. and Rogoff, K. 1983. Empirical exchange rate models for the seventies: Do they fit out of sample? *Journal of International Economics* 14:3-24.

Nappi, Carmine. 1990. *Le Cuivre*. Paris: Economica.

Nappi, Camine. 1994. *L'Aluminium*. Paris. Economica.

Ohlin, Bertil G. 1933. *Interregional and International Trade*. Cambridge, MA: Harvard University Press.

Oppenheim, A. Leo. 1964. *Ancient Mesopotamia, Portrait of a Dead Civilization*. Chicago, IL: University of Chicago Press.

Parker, S. T., and K. R. Gibson 1979. A developmental model for the evolution of language and intelligence in early hominids. *Behavioral and Brain Sciences* 2:367–407.

Pinker, Steven. 1999. *How the Mind Works*. New York: W. W. Norton.

Podolny, Joel and Karen Page. 1998. Network forms of organization. *Annual Review of Sociology* 24:57–76.

Polanyi, Karl. 1944. *The Great Transformation*. New York: Rinehart and Company.

Prebisch, Raul. 1959. Commerical policy in the underdeveloped countries. *American Economic Review* 49:251–273.

Pringle, Heather. 1998. Cradle of cash; When money arose in the ancient cities of Mesopotamia, it profoundly and permanently changed civilization. *Discover* 19:1-10.

Radetski, Marian. 1990. *A Guide to Primary Commodities in the World Economy*. Oxford, Basil Blackwell.

Rauch, James E. 1999. Networks versus markets in international trade. *Journal of International Economics* 48:7–35.

Rauch, James E. and Robert C. Feenstra. 1999. Introduction to symposium on business and social networks in international trade. *Journal of International Economics* 48:3–6.

Rauch, James E. and Alessandra Casella. 2001. *Networks and Markets*. New York: Russell Sage Foundation.

Rauch, J. and Trindade, V. 2002. Ethnic Chinese networks in international trade. *Review of Economics and Statistics* 84:116-30.

Rebuffat, François. 1996. *La Monnaie dans L'Antiquité*. Paris: Picard.

Ridley, Matt. 2000. *Genone: The Autobiography of A Species in 23 Chapters*. New York: Harpers Collins.

Ridley, Matt. 1996. *The Origins of Virtue, Human Instincts and the Evolution of Cooperation*. New York: Penguin Books.

Riley-Smith, *Atlas des Croisades*. Paris: Éditions Autrement.

Rosenberg, Nathan. 1972. *Technology and American Economic Growth*. Armonk, NY: M.E. Sharpe.

Rostovtzeff, M. 1957. *The Social and Economic History of the Roman Empire*. Oxford: Clarendon Press.

Ruffin, Roy J. 1999. The nature and significance of inra-industry trade. *Federal Reserve Bank of Dallas Economic and Financial Review* 2–10.

Samhaber, Ernst. 1963. *Merchants Make History, How Trade has Influenced the Course of the History throughout the World*. London: George G. Harrap.

Schmandt-Besserat, Denise. 1977. An archaic recording system and the origin of writing. *Syro-Mesopotamian Studies* 1–31.

Semmel, Bernard. 1970. *The Rise of Free Trade Imperialism*. Cambridge: Cambridge University Press.

Shreeve, James. 1995. *The Neanderthal Enigma, Solving the Mystery of Human Origins*. New York: William Morrow and Co.

Silver, Morris. 1986. *Economic Structures of the Ancient Near East*. London: Croom Helm.

Silver, Morris. 1995. *Economic Structures of Antiquity*. Westport, CT: Greenwood Press.

Smith, Adam. 1776. *An Inquiry into the Nature and Causes of the Wealth of Nations*. Chicago, IL: Encyclopaedia Britannica.

Sobel, Robert M. 1972. *The Age of Giant Corporations, A Microeconomic History of American Business 1914–1970*. Westport, CT: Greenwood Press.

Solso, Robert L. 1999. *Mind and Brain Science in the 21st Century*. Cambridge, MA: MIT Press.

Starr, Ross and M. Stinchcombe. 1999. Exchange in a network of trading posts," in Chichilnisky, G. (Ed.) *Markets, Information and Uncertainty: Essays in Economic Theory in Honor of Kenneth J. Arrow*. Cambridge, UK: Cambridge University Press.

Suk-Young Chwe, Michael. 2000. Communication and coordination in social networks. *Review of Economic Studies* 67:1-16.

Tooby, John and Leda Cosmides. 1990. The past explains the present: Emotional adaptation and the structure of ancestral environments. *Ethnology and Sociobiology* 11:375–424.

Toutain, Jules. 1930. *The Economic Life of the Ancient World*. New York: Alfred A. Knopf.

Treffler, Daniel. 1993. International factor price differences: Leontief was right! *Journal of Political Economy* 101:961–987.

Trefler, Daniel. 1995. The case of missing trade and other mysteries. *American Economic Review* 85:1029–1046.

Tse-Tung, Mao.1935. *On Tactics against Japanese Imperialism*.

United Nations. 1984. *Industrial Statistics Yearbook 1984*. New York, United Nations.

U.S. Department of Commerce. 1975. *Historical Statistics of the U.S.: Colonial Times to 1970, Bicentennial Edition*. Washington, D.C.: Bureau of the Census.

U.S. Department of Commerce. *Annual Survey of Manufactures*. Washington, D.C.: Bureau of the Census.

U.S. Department of Commerce. 1986. *Survey of Current Business*. Washington, D.C.: Bureau of Economic Analysis.

Vanek, Jaroslav. 1968. The factor proportions theory: The N-factor case. *Kyklos* 21:749–756.

Vanek, Jaroslav. 1972. The natural resource content of foreign trade 1870–1955, and the relative abundance of natural resources in the United States. *Review of Economics and Statistics*.

van Schaik, C. P. 1983. Why are diurnal primates living in groups? *Behaviour* 87: 120-144.

Wei, Shang-Jin. 1996. Intra-national versus international trade: How stubborn are nations in global integration? NBER Working Paper 5531.

Weidenbaum, M. and S. Hughes. 1996. *The Bamboo Network*. New York: The Free Press.

Willliamson, Oliver E. 2000. The new institutional economics: Taking stock, looking ahead. *Journal of Economic Literature* 38:595-613.

Wilson, Edward O. 1998. *Consilience, the Unity of Knowledge*. New York, NY: Vintage Books.

Wrangham, R.W. 1987. The significance of African apes for reconstructing human social evolution. In Kinzey W.G. (Ed.) *Primate Models of Hominid Evolution*. Albany, NY: SUNY Press.

Yi, Kei-Mu. 2003. Can vertical specialization explain the growth of world trade? *Journal of Political Economy* 111.

0-595-33054-1

www.ingramcontent.com/pod-product-compliance
Lightning Source LLC
Chambersburg PA
CBHW021542200526
45163CB00014B/726